The Princess and
the Search for
Pearl
Blake
Harper Nigeria

I0757047

DEDICATION

To all those farmers who were gruesomely murdered by the alleged Fulani Herdsmen in Benue State of Nigeria while in search for daily bread, the true pearls of life and those who may have totally lost track of realities and aiming to still draw hope from the seamlessly hopeless conditions in Nigeria. We win because we gave it another attempt.

ACKNOWLEDGEMENT

To God Almighty for insight. To Nigerian leaders who still have character and competence. To Mr. Daniel Kure for the heart of love to watch young folks grow up to be responsible. To friends for keeping me to think about the future of the youths of Africa. To my family for being the best. To the youths of Africa who keep challenging me for greater height.

AUTHOR'S NOTE

If we could trace the part of greatness on paper, we would discover the trajectories. If only Nigerians and Africans as a whole knew that such trajectories demand focus and right attitude, they would shun evil association that could easily beset them and build according to the pattern shown them in the book of experience. When we walk the path of greatness, we become great after all.

INTRODUCTION

Princess is a character that depicts desperation. Her ways were the ways of Mortal. Her acts were the acts spoiled by mere dreams and aspirations but could it be that another influenced her steps? Time will show! The pearl is the essence of existence, the reason why we all work as we walk the sands of time. It could be wealth, affluence and search for relevance leading to success in life. Man is responsible for the problems he is saddled with; maybe pride and ignorance have made him not to discover the reason. As she searched, she discovered the reason why she had to keep searching but that is not without a cost. Such costs are often scary at first especially when we try to build on the foundation, which was not formidably laid. A building without a foundation cannot stand a skyscraper. We could crash when we get too comfortable at a building without a solid foundation. A Savior is truly needed but let such not come when it is too late and when it finally comes, let discretion play it part to know how to strike when it is red-hot.

CONTENTS

CHAPTER ONE

PRINCESS ON THE SCENE, HOW IT ALL BEGAN

It was such a long night and everyone was enjoying the cold night sleep. Rain began around 1:00am that morning. Waking up in the wee hours, very unusual of Princess who was known as the very first to sleep and the last to wake. At least that was the perception of all who knew her. What could have necessitated such early wake? That would be the exact question in the mind of any member of her family who saw her awake in such early hours of the day. She hurriedly went inside the bathroom as if not taking her bath would attract severe punishment. Her mother who was not in a very deep sleep noticed the unusual sound in the house. She decided to open just one eye in a bid to avoid being caught, as though what she wants to note, will not be worthy of note when seen by an eye. It did not take Princess three minutes to rush out from the bathroom; she would usually take about six minutes to scrub only her back on a normal day when she is not on such fox jump as was seen this faithful day.

As the popular saying goes, *when the usual becomes unusual then there is need to watch out else assumption becomes the normal way of life*. It is becoming obvious that something is fishy; no doubt what is hidden will soon be made manifest. As the wise saying goes that *what a child cannot see standing, an elder will see while sitting down.* Princess went into her room, hurried over her make up like one who has mastered the art of beautification. She moved straight to her wardrobe as one who suddenly picked up quarrel with her clothing. She reached out to one light skimpy black flowing gown and sweat it in her body, dashed out to the mirror so that her beauty would be well seen for the admiration of her peers. A touch here and there was all she needed to fit into the gown like one who is expecting her in-law from far away land. Rushing into her shoe rack, she pulled out a heeled shoe to fit with her black flowing gown. Picking up her elegant bag as if she would not be back for weeks. Wow, a damsel at a glance, a depiction of a true African beauty. This got her mother wondering as her curiosity could no longer be satisfied. A slight cough from her mother scared her as she turned towards where her mother lay down to see if such noise popped open her mother's eyes. She turned to the gazing eye of her mother whose eye contact depicts anger and surprise.

1

1

Eeem! Eeem!! Mummy you are awake already? (She asked just to calm her panting nerves down)

I have been awake for as long as the unusual moves you made kept me! She replied to Princess

Where are you going to this early morning dressed like this? She asked without refusing to remove her gaze at Princess who was already dressed on a sexy flowing gown, displaying such an unusual attitude and looks of anxiety as early as 6.00am on Saturday morning.

Where are you going gladly dressed this early morning? She echoed again but this time with a higher voice tone, without refusing to remove her eyes on Princess's eyes.

Yes mummy! I have been invited for a world-class event where the elites in the society would be attending today and I need to be at my best! Sorry I did not inform you mummy nor did I inform daddy. I was so afraid I could be stopped from going! She said with a tune depicting repentance. *This event was actually organized by his Excellency, the Governor at the State House and for the very first time the Governor has requested to honor all the final year students in my department as a result of our academic new track record and I had always looked forward to such*

opportunity as this,

She replied!

Okay! Be very careful and ensure you maintain moderation as you go! Replied the mother of which Princess obliged happily.

I love you mum, you are the best in Africa! She said smiling.

She rushed out with the speed of light, very happy with expectations beaming on her face as her academic year set have been made the special guests of honor. As she stepped out from their gate after a short while, she saw a cab coming towards the other direction.

Cab! Cab!! She beckoned on him as he stopped at her front.

Take me to the State House at once and I will give you a just reward accordingly! She said.

Hop in! Replied the Cabman

As they drew near the State House, as usual were scattered within the venue heavily armed security men.

Why won't it be expected when the Governor and his entourage are being expected at the banquet and that is not without the company of his wife and children?

As Princess made her way to the entrance of the event, she was accustomed by one of the security men who requested to get her clearance to the event.

Yes! Young girl, can I know you?

Oh! Okay! I am Princess Uchechukwu from department of History and International Relation, the department for whom this event was organized; she replied with a little disappointment on her face as though she would want to slap the man for delaying her with stupid questions.

Can I see your pass code or your permit card to identify that you belong to the claimed department and duly invited?

The pass code sadly she was not aware was shared the very day she left the class before close of school.

Sir, I cannot be here if I do not belong here and beside we were not told to bring such and it is for our sake and our academic prowess that people are gathered here today (that she said thinking such are the striking words needed to grant her access to the banquet hall)

The security man looked at her like one trying to notice something on her body but that was actually an eye of admiration at her breath-taking look but heavily constrained by a sense of duty. Suddenly coming back to his senses again continued by saying,

It is very obvious to me that you are not with any means of identification that could authenticate your claims.

She was furious at the man but reality dawn on her that she might be missing the event and what started as an interesting joke been cracked by the security personnel is becoming a reality to her.

While they were still dragging on whose position stands, she sighted some of her colleagues already seated inside but all were with a tag upon showing their means of identification as requested by the security men whose faces were beclouded with a sense of seriousness to duty.

Not willing to miss the banquet for any reason, she considered rushing back to the house in search for her identity card but that will automatically dash her plans of attending as her father was never in support of such occasions. She was very much aware that the kind of father she has is an ardent preacher of decency and does not support any of his children going for such event.

He had heard stories of how young girls were raped and even killed at such occasions especially when hosted by such personalities in a state. What will she do now? She thought to herself like one hallucinating and crossing the thin demarcation between sanity and insanity already.

She began to plead with the security man promising to do anything so long as she does not miss the banquet which may be a onetime opportunity in her life to sit with the high and mighty in the society and have such an experience and a good report she would like to share with her friends, family and children for posterity sake.

But all her plea and effort was futile as the security man was bent on doing the right thing.

Who would rescue her? How would she get a savior to access the event? It would only take the Governor to save her of the embarrassment and mockery she would face going home without having any story to tell upon her early rise and almost not having enough rest for the night.

All her lifelines were already exhausted as the person that will be her only savior was already inside the banquet hall making merry and enjoying the well decorated atmosphere and with the help of a cool music, was driving home the food and exotic drinks into his stomach with all the high and mighty seated inside the banquet hall.

As she was wondering outside, it dawned on her the realities on ground. While she was pondering what to do, how to maneuver her way, as restless as a pregnant woman who was left alone at her distress, she figured out a puzzle but that will not be necessary until she could decode the writings on the wall. A code may be necessary to find her way but the writing must be interpreted to the understanding of the security men to be able to pass.

THE PEARL

The pearls of life no doubt is very necessary and the search must begin immediately. The effectiveness of every search is the knowledge of what is lost. When what is lost is not known, the assurance of a successful search cannot be ascertained. Pearl is something costly, classy and cherish by all and whosoever finds it, have found a treasure indeed. The pearl as used in this book is figurative to denote the precious things of life. Everybody wants to live a fulfilled life with all the best things of life, which include: wealth, affluence, influence, respect, honor, good health and sound education. Any man who enjoys all these is said to be very successful because that is what the world seeks as an interpretation for all the commitments to life. When pearl is used in this book, it denotes life filled with abundance of happiness, joy and satisfaction as a result of attaining certain societal standards. This life's journey Princess began in search for relevance, success and happy ever after will be judged successful when all these have been found.

CHAPTER TWO

THE JOURNEY

What must I do now? Said the Princess in a thought mixed with agony after the disappointment at the event. How do I tell the story? She kept on thinking loud. When a thought becomes loud, even the gods could no longer hold the centre. We live in the reality when we become victims of what we preach. Princess was always known as the loud one, especially when she is in the midst of her friends at school.

One time at school, she created a scene in the class, when she wanted to prove a point to her mates during a lecture. She rose up in the class and began to challenge what her teacher said in the class with the intention to demean him. That did not go well with the teacher and he became very angry with Princess and asked that she walk out of the class, she refused but instead began to threaten to expose the lecturer of his sexual assaults on the female students in the class. That was the beginning of branding her as the black sheep of the class. Is it not obvious the reason why she was not even aware of the pass code given for the occasion, which she was supposed to attend with her mates at the State House? The expectation now is to seek for the written code which would help her get all that was given as information and benefits to all those who participated in the banquet hosted by the Governor and inside this piece of information is found the way to the pearls of life which includes how to be relevant in the society, affluence, wealth, health and comfort. As the saying goes that he who plays the piper dictates the tone, so also was the time to device a means to getting the same entitlement. Entitlement is not the product of title but responsibility and that unknown to Princess, is the reason why crown befits the head that wears it. An adage which says that a *child who fails to correct what made an elder useless, will soon pass through what the elder passed through to become useless*. If the pearl is something valuable, then people who are valuable through a processed character must manage it. On the day Princess came into the family some scenarios played out that brought about her name. There was an expectation for a female child from her parent who had given birth to male children in all. The father had always wanted a female child who would take care of him at his old age as the African tradition demands. He was not a happy man at all after long years of waiting and was ready to do anything to have a female child. Her mother was not so bothered though would not say no when such gift comes. African women have this calmness when it comes to responsibility of childbirth at least they understand the pains and joy of child bearing. After a long wait, they decided to garner advices from some elders who would not mind giving solutions no matter the repercussion. They were advised to adopt a female child. Well that would not be breaking news after all many families do so, they told the parents of Princess. That decision did not sink well with the father of Princess but as the saying goes that *when the desirable is not available, the available should become the desirable*, they swiftly jumped at the decision without further probing.

In Africa, adopting a child is very legal so long as it is done in a very legal way but one disadvantage of adopting a child is the genetic makeup of the offspring to be adopted which may certainly affect the behavior of the child subsequently. Biological science has helped us to understand that the behavior of a child is dependent on the genetic makeup and the environment where the child is raised. One could say that such factors play important role on character formation of a child but to what factor we can attribute that of Princess, time will unveil. The name Princess was given to her because of how beautiful she is when she was adopted. The father was filled with joy and called her Princess, the name she eventually bore till date. But one would think that the name of a child should affect the behavior of the child but that was not the case of Princess and has never been the case of any in Africa, as she acts so clumsy and silly most times. But the father loved her and was willing to do anything to make her happy. When she passed out from high school and was ready to go for her University education, she decided to study History and International Relation. That was the happiest moment in the family as her father could not hold his joy and hence provided everything to make her happy including buying her anything good as he comes back from work or any official outing. That made Princess very excited and overtly spoilt. She often thinks that her beauty alone is enough to give her anything she wants without knowing that the beauty of every woman is her character as well as that of any man.

In Africa, we celebrate more of the beauty within than the physical beauty, that is beauty without. We cannot truly tell how far a woman could go until we can tell how much well behaved she is. That would be the yardstick to even decide whom she could be betrothed to for marriage. Princess grew up in the time when a young damsel is betrothed to a promising young man even before she could learn to judge between good and bad. How did her search for relevance began seeing that the finding of the required pearl will usher in a mark of true relevance to her? Let the search begin!

CHAPTER THREE

THE NEXT LEVEL

Few days at school after the banquet hosted by the Governor for all the students of History and International Relation, the students were all happy at least what they have always yearn for is now a reality and everyone has a story to take home. There is a need to face life since the new graduates would soon emerge that would be expected to proffer solutions to the numerous needs in Africa. Africa is a continent endowed with both human and natural resources, in a serene environment. We have the best human resources but the leadership styles of her leaders have ravaged the continent, leaving it prone to anarchy. In Africa, we have the ability to lead the world when we learn how to learn ourselves. To be able to judge disobedient, we must ensure that our obedience is complete and that is where we have missed it. We have mastered the art of playing 'Big Brother' role to other continent, leaving out the responsibility of being our brother's keeper in Africa. This again is an error and strives under the wind, so says the preacher. Princess having missed the event was not happy but like the popular saying goes, *the stubbornness of a he goat does not excuse it from being dragged to the market place*. It is one thing to get education and yet another to be truly educated. To be educated is to be able to solve problems without using the same mentality that created them. That has always been the problem of African Leaders hence much is expected from the graduated class Princess belongs. They are expected to be creative and respect the societal norms. That is expected from any one who would be a leader in the 21st century seeing that the 21st century greatest resource is no longer oil but human capacity. Realities are beginning to unfold to Princess as she later was told that the search for relevance began at that very banquet she missed, which the Governor of her state organized for them. Education may only be a relief from ignorance when the drops of water gotten from it are not consistent to make a mighty ocean. That implies that the educated mind must be a real asset not a liability to the nation. Life at final year is often characterized with seemingly basking in the euphoria of the moment without a thought on life to be after school.

The quest for relevance for some people begins after school but to the wise, such plans must be properly arranged and kept to mind for any serious person during school and then rolled out sequentially after school. If a vision is not well scripted in the tablets of our heart and even a step further in a book, it cannot form the compass for a successful race in life. Wise people write their vision and make it plain upon tables so that they that read may run with it. Princess was not aware of the realities outside school. Back in the days, every student looked forward to matriculating into higher institution and is not in a hurry to think about the convocation. Such attitude is a myopic view that has kept Africa almost at the lowest ebb of development when measured with the developmental strides in other continents. So with the lack of urgency in the heart, the environment would soon silence all the aspirations and dreams after school, only for them to be taken unawares that soon their days would be numbered. They often get so unprepared for graduation when they matriculated because they assume that education is the end itself and not the means to an end. Princess and some of her mates were not left out in this web circle. We can only attain relevance when we have built enough character to maintain where we wish to remain and to Princess, relevance is a matter of inheritance from parents and not a function hard work. How long can inherited asset last when we do not master its usage? That was the question any one who wish to feature in the future must first picture. On that faithful day, when Princess wrote her last paper, she had a cold bath, jubilation was in the air and everyone was looking forward to one night with the governor after all her academic year made the best result in the entire school and that is deafening enough for celebration. The best celebration is the celebration for the right success. What truly defines success? Success is attaining a set mark, surpassing expectations of others with character to maintain it. That was also not taken into account by Princess and many of her mates. This equally as seen today has kept Africa in the lowest ebb of development with all her scintillating natural endowments. When people begin to see success as that which should affect the society at large, the norm of selfishness begins to fizzle out giving way to selflessness.

We often neglect the training of our character, which is not given any course code in the higher institutions of learning. We often pay more attention in acquiring academic certificates without getting enough character and right principles to use it. So while we seem to breed empty minds in a loaded head as students, we sometimes breed people who are eloquent but not able to replicate in others what they know. Ability of the mind is as important as the ability of the head and when one is grossly neglected, development is mortgaged. Princess believed that education is only a training of the head and little was given into development of her character and competence, which are the require ingredients for societal relevance. How did we get here? One would ask! Why did we get here? Another would ask. The quest must begin for the pearl to be found and the discovery of the pearl begins with the discovery of self.

CHAPTER FOUR

THE SEARCH BEGAN

When Princess left the scene of the event that very day, she as well as other students went for the search of what would mark the beginning of true relevance for them. They may have gotten the idea of what the pearl looks like at the event but that does not translate into having the pearl. What is know and not used is not different from what is not known. Everyone desires true relevance but eventually many do not get to find it and those who found it, may not be able to truly decode it. Princess was determined but how far would her determination take her? We would know.

Finding a written code, yet to be decoded that appeared to be hidden for ages, only God knows for how long, Princess had mixed feelings. What on earth could be going on in her mind? That must be a sign of happiness as her face was beaming with such suggestion as though that is what she has been searching for ages. The happiness as was learnt from her countenance was because finally she would know the direction to go after graduation, having waited with eagerness. This is the decision that would obviously enlist her for relevance. Path to career fulfillment is first the knowledge of what aligns with our gift and talent and the ability to refine it and use it effectively to create wealth and impact generations.

What appeared to be the long painful silence after graduation would be decoded and many would soon know their stand as to what they are to gain from life outside school. They will understand what the future holds but since the mixed feelings were still there, suddenly sadness spread like wide cotton again on her face, as the code was yet to be decoded. It is sure not enough to find a solution but to know how to appropriate the solution found is where the bulk of work is. But being found is better than remaining encoded, she thought to herself, since it is found it is half way solved as a problem. Who would not feel same after what appeared to be age longed waiting from when she matriculated till now? It is this kind of waiting that reveals the character one had deliberately built during and after school. Such character is what the world outside school looks for which shows forth how relevant a man would be even when he is employed. The next question going on in her mind is how to clear the doubt over the empire nature had accumulated for men on earth and how everyone could take a piece of the cake from the generous wealth of nature. This is the very reason why it appears that some people are more equal than others in the society because any man who finds it will rule others.

We have been on a long suffering and was left with what is required to take care of us, when we decide to work hard and be diligent at whatever choice we make in life, Princess thought to herself.

Such feeling of a lady who have been caged in the four walls of the university only to be release to access the enormous wealth available within the confines of his environment and suddenly discovered she is not prepared to access them. I remember such feelings when we kept thinking that a jump into the labor market of the society would be a sudden jump into the national wealth and asset.

Oftentimes the entitlement mentality makes many half-baked graduates, with certificate that cannot certify their inert abilities and character. Before now, Princess had calculated the number of buildings and cars she would buy but all have remained like building a castle in the air. The pains have lingered for long with no one to cushion the effect and worst of it is the bullying by lecturers and parents, who just think that the consistent scolding of a child is the antidote against stupidity if the child thinks otherwise. *What then is the benefit of having around you what you have no or little access to?* Princess said louder to herself as one hallucinating already and crossing the demarcation between sanity and insanity. The newfound mystery has attracted the attention of all but it is still encoded. The mystery is the inequalities that exist in the society where the rich gets richer and the poor gets poorer. *There must be a reason for this*, Princess thought. Could it be that what we get in life is based on what we do in life? Could it be that nature is unfair and bias to give fortune to those it likes and withholds fortune from those it hates?

Princess was worried, because she had many ugly experiences with her teachers and was labeled as a very disobedient student who was always bent on doing what she wanted. As she was going along the road, she got to where people gathered, the muttering audience were just watching and waiting for what life could offer, pairing were noticed, while discussions were going lower as though the air would be angry hearing it. The kind of talk that even the deaf nodes in acceptance was such as heard amidst the expectant folks until it disappeared completely. This was so much disturbing as you could easily hear the sound of a pin when it dropped. An elder will nod and hear the sound of his nodding while children could read the minds of the elders who have gathered. Indeed, words are parables and only the discerning can master the use.

I am beginning to love the silence, a man whispered in the ear of another man, who sat to observe life and the things it offers. *How can you be enjoying what others were panicking about replied the man?* That must be from depth of revelation that there is nothing hidden that will not be made manifest though it tarries. There is something relevant and influential the rich people know that the poor people do not know. Everyone was expectant and that is the kind of expectation that could keep the dead worried even. Why won't the dead be worried when they are uncertain also of where they are going? When a journey seems unending, even a lad suspects his father and that is found in the 'book of experience'. If we are to fathom by sampling the heart beat of everyone the environment on the uncertainties of life, the rate of their heart beat is enough to chase a young lad back into a mother's couch or better still correct a deaf ear.

After what seems to be a long waiting, shortly the atmosphere was saturated with a distant but gradually approaching voice as a crying Angel, wailing over his lost heartthrob. Such myth and legend stories told of old of how a betrothed virgin will not sleep until her husband returns from hunting squirrel at twilight. Immediately, the pairing whispering that was heard before gradually silenced as though there was another emergency on ground demanding urgent attention. You know when there are two conditions demanding urgent attention, the most critical one is given the first attention. Soon the voice becomes clearer as it approaches closer. It became obvious that such a voice is not to be ignored for when the gong sounds repeated, then there is need for even the elders to listen and attend to matters of utmost importance. A true elder will be required to lend his voice at the community hall when issues that bothers his pocket is being discussed especially when his rivalry is in opposition to him. A man contesting for a chieftaincy title does not smile at his rivalry on the day of coronation. Such meeting as was seen does not need distraction from a little child who needs to eat roasted yam at home. What again happened? Princess asked! The imaginations could be seen from the eyes of the people who where discussing the issues of life. *Something must have happened* thought some eager-gathered multitude waiting to know the next step for life just as Princess waited. *It could be that the mystery will soon become a thing of the past* said another.

It is the dawn of a new horizon and the break of a new day. The way to relevance is in the discovery of the pearl and the knowledge of its usage. Soon the doubt was cleared in the minds of the people, as a voice suddenly approaching ahead, ushering what has thrown many in doubt about life. Immediately, the hidden mystery was unveiled and it was discovered that a good character is the building ladder to future relevance. This is what has kept many in the dark since and few are they, which take cognizance of it. Oftentimes, small things are not actually small because the means of getting it may be big and the big thing may appear small depending on the approach towards it. A wise man that wishes to attain relevance must first of all decide to count the cost. This is the mystery and that is the awaited understanding towards the search for the pearls of life.

CHAPTER FIVE

THE OMITTED STEP

Lets trace the trajectory to know where the water went soar for Princess. Where did she miss it and how did she miss it? Growing up during her High School, Princess had learnt a lot about the University and the opportunities it offers. She could no longer wait to experience all she had learnt and heard about the University. Little wonder her favorite moment was when she watch campus related movies, that showed off the 'happening babes' as they are fondly called, who would wear all the show off dresses and posit their cleavages to attract and catch the 'sugar ants" who would be bent on nothing but to have a taste. Being very good looking, she had hoped to trap many male lecturers and make them beg on their knees for her wet lips and curved figure. One wonderful thing about the University as many have come to discover is that it plays along with any kind of lifestyle one choses to live, without restricting any choice. Nobody cares to know what you do and how you do it so long as it does not violate the school rules and regulations.

University is a place where you would find your fellow mavericks and weirdoes depending on what brought you to school. It is true because different reasons abound for different people why they came to the school. To some, it is to tour on the serene environment of the University while to others, it is to make friends. Lecture time is always awesome as many came to learn and others came to distract people who would want to learn. What we get from the experience is what we decided to commit into doing. Princess felt it would be a smooth ride since she had thought that it is a matter of nice physic and shape. Princess failed to appreciate the fact that it takes right decisions to walk to work. One greatest weapon available to everyone is decision, it is an individual property right. Sometimes it could be very tough especially when hard work and determination is the only access way to success. It would take a lot of burnt midnight candles to get something out of the University. Each time she stayed glued to the Television, her parent would always scold her with words like, *If you continue to watch people on the television, nobody will be able to watch you eventually.* Those words hurt like fire in the ears of Princess since that was contrary to what she wants to hear. Often times she would mutter words as she walks away angrily from the presence of her parents especially her mother who does not derive joy to watch her father pamper her too much. *She is still a little girl*, her father would always insist when her mother becomes so hard at her. But training is not sweet at all because it takes sweat to enjoy the sweet things of life. There are times when you wonder if the endless nights of stress, toils and occasional despair of life are worth the time and money we invest into attaining success.

Many times we are quick to throw in the towel only to forget that the shadow of a man is an indication of the presence of the man. We may not be where we want to be but sure, we are not where we used to be. Such is always the journey of a man whose aim is at creating lasting relevance in time and eternity. You may also be dismayed because you feel as if you have not quite figured out 'adulting' or what it means to be successful. We do not take time to understand that life is in stages. There are times when we got all our bills paid and there are times when we are required to pay our bills. We may not understand the struggles of life since we are yet to figure out how to pay bills, buy a house or car, navigate the world of job handling but sure these are very real. It is responsibility that matures a man while it takes pressure to prove the worth of a man. What Princess failed to find out was how real in reality these responsibilities could be. But truly these are steps to relevance in life. These realities dawned on many students in Africa after school, when they came to understand that there are many differences between smiling at something and smiling with something.

Education would teach a man what success is and may not tell him how success is attained, that is a call being responsible could make, a demand placed on the true pearls of life. So to be responsible is a choice we must teach our conscience to make without a bias move. The future will always respond to decision to being responsible. A mere futile thought on the future could freak out someone who is not quite ready to enter the harsh reality of the job market, to assume the responsibilities of being a responsible person and embrace the cold world that fluctuates. Education is a basic requirement to success but it takes consistency to arrive at success destination.

The major difference between a successful man and a failed man is not opportunity alone but the thought of not being sure to make an impact in life. Especially in these days of uncertainty when professional courses are not a guarantee to being successful in life, responsibility is required. Princess also thought the same while she was about pursuing a career at school, building her castles only in the air with sweet imaginations of what it would be like being a celebrity but unknown to her planning is imminent upon her responsibility if success is a focus. All these aforementioned thoughts in the mind of Princess could be seen as ridiculous, when not matched with requisite responsibility but sure reality will also catch up with many who coated success with frivolities and sure time would reveal.

I am sure many if not all could attest to the fact that what we failed to pick up on our aspirations for the top, we would meet on our way down. The waterloo we would find would be an indication that the pearl was what we least bargained for. The value of the pearl, the dog may not know and the price they may trample on the ground because value is not in the container alone but in the content thereof.

Men who figure out their purpose for life are destined to use their gifts and talents to create lasting relevance if they could take a fearless responsibility of life, devoid of distractions.

Princess was a high flier but not with the attitude of subliming values and allowing it become a mirage. Any commitment we make towards becoming a better person is worth the stress and the hard work because the future is not featured until it is picture with the intent to fix it to the taste we want it. Dreams are not meant to be mere dreams for long; they can be activated to fly high above, transcending imaginations. There is no true fruit without first being made to bud and that is a process and precept of time. We are not meant to break responsibilities entrusted to us with unalloyed brittle since it leads to age longed relevance. We are not given to flake out on our dreams but like a wise hen, incubate it to maturity with responsibility for the time, discipline and sacrifice given to it.

Many people who failed to take full responsibilities on what they want often resolve to push blame on people and that is a clear evidence of weakness, not being ready for what they truly want from life.

When Princess came out from the university, it dawned on her that out of school does not amount to being ready for the world. Success is defined as both an inward and outward preparation meeting opportunity. Princess began to apportion blame on the school she attended for not teaching her all she needed to know, to her parent for not telling her what to do and to her friends for taking her out of her ways from realities of life but these are not equals wisdom. Wisdom is taking full responsibility of how our life plays out. It is seeing the pit holes that trapped others and refusing to willfully give into it. When we are able to decipher judgments and people's opinion then can we truly be said to have prepared for the cost of relevance.

CHAPTER SIX

THE SOARED APPLE

When we see roadblocks on our journey of life, a wise decision would often be to stop and ponder how best to cross it. That may be judged as delay but the wise understands that the beginning of success is a wise decision and right counsel. Where there is wise counsel, wars are won. Princess was not aware of the state of moral decadence ravaging the society where she found herself. Level of indecency ravaging the society has made living a decent life almost outdated but it is not hopeless. How would she know, when she is also caught in the same web?

While growing up, she had a lot of environmental influences, being the only girl in the family, pampered to a fault; she did not take into account her lifestyle. The web of societal influence is often very strong, when bad system; bad people and bad decisions surround us. How did it all start for Princess, having attended the best school in town?

It was already 6pm on a Friday, over 12hours she left home for an errand and her parents had not seen her stay out that late. She had some house chores to do and the uneasiness associated with her being the only female child of the family makes it very difficult for her mother to allow her stay late away from home. *"What must have kept her so long away from home''* her mother wondered. *"But she never told us of any friend around the home where she must have visited"*, she thought with worry filling her heart. Princess' fault was not only that she left the home but also that she left for so long without informing anyone of her where about. Whilst in her mother's wondering, her phone rang, looking through the screen, she saw it was unknown number calling;

"Hello mummy, it is Princess and I am very sorry that I am calling to inform you late, I had to get to school to pick up my handout, which I forgot, I'll be home in the next 45minutes please"

Princess pleaded on the other side of the line. *"It is alright, be very careful and ensure you don't stay longer than you said"*, her mother replied. When parents begin to allow their children to do anything they like without stern caution then that might be a high way to the grave. Princess had followed some of her friends to a party, where they introduced her to another way of life. She was coarse to experience the so-called 'big life' where she was given cigarette and hard drinks to taste. That was the beginning of her problems in life. No doubt when the saying goes, *"evil communication will ruin good manners"*. Princess was the hunt of every young man in town who knows 'what's up' because of her charming looks. She is very fair in color with attractive contours projecting and well standing breast like a fixed standard balls. Her sexy eyes would keep every guy wondering and even cost such a man lost of consciousness for minutes. That day was the beginning of her dark life.

While she was at the party, she got introduced to sex and foreplay as an evidence of maturity. Youths of these days experiment all things to learn even when it could be at the detriment of their future. She got entangled with this bad life, a cancer that ate her up to character deformation. Princess had a bite of the golden apple and became addicted to such forbidden apple. Sex is like a coated scorpion, which does not recognize the owner and can sting without mercy. She began to hunt for any man she could see just to make up with him. It was like a hobby for her and it looked like the devil was using this juicy trap to destroy her destiny and thwart her aspirations. Sex has a way of suspending reasoning because when the urge comes, it drives blood to the sex organs and pulse all creativity for good works. At that stance, no sufficient blood pumps to the brain because a large percentage of the blood supplies to the reproductive part. Amidst the lustful ecstasy Princess enjoyed at the party on that day, something struck her mind and she noticed that the time had been far spent at the party. Certainly feared gripped her on what would be the reaction of her parents when she gets home. Gosh! She exclaimed! She had promised her mother to be home in the next 45minutes and it been past 1hour. She thought of what next to do but her high headedness could not articulate anything and already she was drunk. No option came to her head but to simply go home to face the music since she had long practiced the steps to the music she would face at home; the music of cause and effect. With her heart filled with guilt and sadness, she headed home but the seed had already been planted waiting to grow forthwith. When a child learns the practice it took to bring her to the world on time, she would think that it is the only way to go in the world. Princess felt that the world revolves around her so fast as to crumble on her. When she got home, her waiting parents, who like a toothless bulldog only barked without cogent actions taken to forestall the future occurrence, welcomed her. Well, nothing corrective was done and no stringent measures taken. So that is a license for the next steps to practice for Princess.

There is certainly no character that is learnt overnight. It begins with a little action either neglected or encouraged by the people around. I said neglected in a stance where it is a bad seed planted through the negative companies we keep, or encouraged in the stance where it is a good seed planted through right behaviors from people around us. There is nobody who was born bad or good but what we consistently do, we become. There is no training that is not costly and the only thing not costly is assumption that life is only a function of academic certificates when building of good character is not a deliberate life commitment. Princess began this dark character in a day and became addicted to that kind of life and that was the beginning of her stumbling block.

CHAPTER SEVEN

THE TREASURED PEARL

Africa is known as the citadel for excellence at least every can-do spirit is resident in the continent of Africa. One of the most beautiful paraded assets in Africa is our women. The black race is often known as naturally endowed with creativity, wisdom to do and create and happy is such a man who finds a woman who is beautiful from inside out. All this while, Princess had thought that life of relevance begins and ends with paper certificate, which is able to show what a person can do even when the person is unable to do such things. Pearl to us, is a cherished commodity, one that is very costly and scarce to get. 21st century is no longer celebrated because of the natural resource found therein but because of the human endowments raised therein. The capacity of any continent is judged by the capacity of her people. These people are seen as pearls when the presence they manifest is able to solve problems and the absence of their presence create vacuums. Education of the head is not enough to confront the challenges of 21st century. We cannot solve a problem with the same mentality that created them, which has always been the benchmark that has caused the continent to live beyond the expectations of the whole world.

When Princess was growing up, her parent was not able to pay attention to the content of her character so long as her physical beauty stands projected. At first Africa saw beauty as the container without content but that has changed long time ago. As the world began to evolve, the true pearl was not found on the container but the content found therein. Such content is the envy of all and hence the earnest desire for any person with foresight to hunt for it. If what we are looking for in a person does not live beyond such person, then it is not an asset for posterity sake.

The entirety of this pearl is wrapped up in one word known as character. I have often wondered why the word character is used to refer to alphabets and numerical. The answer is not far fetch with the conditional demand for relevance.

Princess wants to be relevant but the basic requirements were not considered. I remember one time when she was pointed to the way she treats elders. She did not consider such corrections but her reply was that she owes not one an explanation on how she decides to live her life. That again was neglected even when it was pointed to her parent given that she was the only girl and the *"touch not"* mark given to her by her father was seen as a divine mandate.

I have often asked the reason why alphabets and numbers are called 'characters'. Alphabets are known as characters because the alphabet 'A' would always be the same at any given point in time in any location it is found. The number '1' remains the same every minute of the day in any place. They are not influenced by location, culture, background or climate. This consistency amounts to the level of relevance an alphabet or number gets when used anywhere. That is the hallmark of the trust reposed on these English alphabets and Arithmetical numbers. The formation of our being should be patterned to the consistency in our behavior and that is the prime of life's achievements. We cannot talk about character without consistency. As a matter of fact, it is consistency that breeds trust and what we repeatedly do, we become.

We must begin to note those qualities and features that make us different and build on them. Comparative advantage is the reason why values are place on things and people. What we have and are able to do is the reason why we would be sought for in times of need.

Growing up for Princess was happy news to her parents especially to her daddy, because she was seen as the apple of everybody's eyes that came in contact with her. One of her strong forces is her homely nature and her hardworking prowess at home. Princess was a perfect blend of synergy and empathy, a true essence of African woman. Hard work to her was a commitment, which she is sold out to. Chores at home were work over for her and that made the family very happy. She is able to know what should be done and at the blink of an eye, she gets them done.

Sometimes, her parents deliberately left the management of the home to her, knowing that it is safe at the best hands. She was very creative at things to the amazement of all. Little wonder she became the favorite of the home and that made her father shower her with much gifts. We often do not take time to build on our comparative advantages, which is very important. We would give it up to the mother of Princess who would always insist that Princess gives attention to house chores because every successful marriage begins with flawless home management. In Africa, the way to every man's heart is through his stomach. A man can do anything to a woman who knows the secret to satisfying his stomach. Princess' mother knew this secret even before she got married and that was the magic she used to keep her home peaceful and she would do all things possible to pass the same secret to her daughter. Trust me, Princess learnt that very well. Relevance in life can be truncated when these basic things are not put into action. Character produces trust and trust yields commitment and commitment when fully matured gives birth to work which breed rewards. The only problem Princess had, which also is the chief to her character deformation was her wrong choice of association, which was not tamed at first until it corrupted her altitude and her character building, which was not held at high esteem.

But something must be done to salvage the situation if she would end well.

CHAPTER EIGHT
THE SPACE FOR SPICE

When Princess was growing up, she often gets confused when she watches her mother prepare meals for the family. Among the things that get her attention is often the white substance her mother would always put into the meal to taste. She always wondered why it must be added on every single meal and that would always be the game changer. One day, Princess could no longer hold it any longer and then she asked her mother, the essence of the white substance she always add to meal while cooking, to which her mother told her.

"Princess, she said with smiles beaming on her face, that thing you saw me add is called salt and it is added to bring out the taste of the meal and can also serve as a preservative", she replied.

That was enough to motivate Princess at least she now knows that the white substance her mother always use during cooking is called salt. What was unknown to her was why it is also called preservative and so she asked. To which her mother replied *"Preservatives are the things that are used to keep something longer than the shelve life to avoid spoilage or decay"*. Ever since that day, Princess was always looking for salt while cooking and when she wants to keep something away from spoilage over a longer period, she would simply salt it. One day she went and salted her remaining meal and that made the food salty and when she was asked, she insisted she was trying to preserve the meal to which her parents laughed over it. But she had learnt the lesson that salt is a preservative.

Just as salt is used to preserve food and spice up the taste, pearls are also supposed to be preserved from lost, theft or damage. Pearls are very precious and hence the need to preserve it. When Princess lost her great attitude as a result of wrong association, she knew and saw the effects after her graduation from the University. Who would have thought that all is not about acquisition of academic certificate after repeatedly hearing that all it takes to get all we would want in life is academic certificates. That aspiration was dashed when realities dawned on Princess after school, as she discovered that it is easier to preserve a pearl than to lose it. That did not go well with her since life during school is not the same as life after school. Most times, we are tempted to think that the way our needs are met during school would be the way they would after school. That could lead to utter frustration when we can only imagine such without seeing the reality of it.

Life is a function of responsibility and maturity is also a function of responsibility. It is our responsibility to grow with the knowledge we have garnered from the information at our disposal. It is also our responsibility to mature through the information we also have. What we are responsible for is what generates the values we desire to get. Everything valuable is priceless and costly. To this end, there is a need to protect it. We can only have the deliverables we have paid for and that is also applicable to the things we get out of life. Characters are like pearls which when not carefully protected, they dent our identity and hence the cost of reclaiming it may be high to pay.

Remember that what cost Princess her priceless pearl was her unchecked association with the wrong people. So what it took her to lose it is the same thing it will take her to gain it among other things. One negative thing about bad association is that those involved in assassinating people's character will only tell you the benefits if there are but the repercussions are often hidden from the victims. Everyone wants to be influential, popular, relevant and notable but the shortcuts to these things are often the longest cut to follow. There is a process to life and the things of life. The process it takes to be relevant is a gradual process, which few often neglect at the pursuit of relevance only to crash-land eventually with little or nothing to fall back at. We often want the easy way out of life's already established process. Such easy ways are often a cobra's hole in disguise. We may not see that death is found inside the hole.

Princess thought it was all about having fun and belonging to the high class of life, without knowing that the way to the top is through down.

Association is like a ladder; it can either take us up or bring us down depending on the direction of life we want to follow. The good thing about life is that it is very generous to offer to any man what is chosen out from it. Whatever we desire from life is found in life and wherever we intend to get to in life have once been attained by someone. People who often desire to aspire greater height would always look out for the direction already created by someone who had gone that route before. Precious things are not often found in a seeming favorable environment and so it demand a consistent and persistent search, the bitter truth many do not like to hear. Such search demands that distractions are kept away from us, be it from friends, family or environment. Distractions were the very reason Princess got derailed from the building blocks that would have given her an edge among her equals if she had focused on building character away from distractions of life.

In preserving the pearl, there are various principles to imbibe on. If only Princess had known these principles, perhaps, she would have ended well. Recall that she was not able to attend the graduation party organized by the Governor because her character, which was not built, distracted her from the requirement that would allow her entry into the event venue. Many are like Princess today; they pay more attention to gathering academic certificates, maintaining physical beauty without building character. These they did as a result of wrong influence. But we may not so much blame Princess without looking at the failure of parenting. Children learn more from the unspoken actions of their parents. They may not master the words but the actions speak a lot. A suckling would always look at the face of her mother when she bites the nipple of her mother. That means they know that something had gone wrong especially when a reactions comes from their mother. At that time if they get away with such action without any corrective reaction from their mothers, they would build on such character and gradually they would learn how to be firm at doing wrong things without giving much attention to the repercussions accrued to taking such actions.

Parenting could also be a sure way to preserving the pearl of good character. A child who gets to know the advantage of early training gets to appreciate it at the latter stage of life. Training may be painful, as it does not come without a cost to pay. Such cost may be costly at first but the effect after all is enormous. Pearls are often expensive and hence require expensive measures to preserving it. It may cost much more than its value but the sincere endurance to attaining the value is worth a while, Princess began a life not knowing that training could also be self-acquired.

There is no justifiable excuse given to excuse failure. The world does not celebrate excuse in lieu of success. There is nobody who is given to excuses that would ever actualize dreams and aspirations. The reasons many give for not working out things are the same reason many deploy to achieve success. There is nothing as frustrating as associated with someone who is filled with excuses. That a child is not aware of the pains fire comes with would not excuse such a child from being burnt by fire when trampled upon. That we are not told of the effect of losing the pearl would not preserve the pearl when it is not valued.

CHAPTER NINE

PRINCIPLES FOR PRINCIPALS

What Princess did not understand and never gave attention to learning, is the principles for preserving the pearl.

It was that faithful day when a little enjoyment became a major cost to pay. In the midst of young men and ladies who thronged the terrain to get a bit of what they referred to an enjoyment. Such little time spent on frivolities has often been the hard hit of regrets many lived with for the rest of their years. What must have come over princess to think that principles are only for the principals? Often we are confused to believe life does not subscribe to principles. Since the campus was a free zone where many freestyle their flaunts at the expense of their future, Princess would not mind attending all the parties at school since that was all that gave her an edge over her equals. At least she would have a chance to sit with the so-called *'happening guys in the campus'*. Since she was used to following her hearts, she would sneaked out from her room to attend parties and when she felt she could be caught, she would tip anyone standing on her way to attending the events. This, she was used to doing before her father got such report and decided to keep her under close surveillance.

One of these days, unknown to her parent, she sneaked out to a mega fiesta her course mate had invited her, which she saw was an opportunity to enjoy her life. But whether such was the way to go or not would be made known soon.

She had always fed her ear with how interesting the fiesta could be since it would offer her the opportunity to display her new dance steps, flowing like a monthly period of a woman. It was even worst since she heard that some notable musical celebrities would flood the event. Her evil course mates had always mocked her on the dangers of being a decent and naïve girl as they often said she was, which does not always go well with Princess. But as a girl who is always trying to prove a point, she would do anything to remove her name from such a list as used to differential the happening girls from those who are naïve.

That was the beginning of troubles to Princess having neglected the warnings of her parents on the dangers of teenage pregnancy. They only made mention of it each time they were trying to dissuade her from bringing shame to the family but did not teach her the importance of chastity as a young girl and all round sex education. Sex education is always a forbidden topic in many families, leaving the children at the mercy of media and peer pressures, which many are not well equipped to overcome. Whatsoever children do not learn from home, they may learn in a wrong way since the society is conditioned to teach them what they want them to know and not what they should know. There is a difference between what we want to know and what we should know. What we should know are what we sincerely need to be successful but what we want to know are those things that peer pressures may force us to experiment especially when it has been hyped beyond what it truly is. A lady with great abilities and a very glossy appearance in the eyes of many suddenly became the talk of many as a bad breed. Something must have been missed as a principle.

Principles are those morals we hold at high esteem, which dictate our way of life. They are practiced overtime depending on the information we have about such standards and that eventually become to us a way of life. For instance honest, dedication, commitment, right association are among the principles many hold dear to them, which eventually form the compass through which life's journey becomes a smooth ride. What suddenly came over princess is the same reason why an excellent student would suddenly become a mockery to the society. It is the same reason why a one time respected girl would suddenly become a whitewashed sepulcher. Why would Princess cast her pearls to swine, desiring to mortgage her future for a little enjoyment? This is the Princess who has always been the glory of her parent, being the only girl of the family, and Eagle among Ducks and the little star the shines among the galaxies. It was crystal clear that all eyes were on her to deliver the goods she had been sent to the University to buy but instead she changed the order to what suits her and her environment. When the right principles are neglected, surely the dice is cast. How did Princess come to believe that there are no longer other ways to be a celebrity than to cast her pearl to a swine? How could she even think that the route to relevance is through shortcuts? These are questions begging for answers, when Princess failed to keep the principles that could preserve her pearls.

Something must have gone wrong in her perspective of life and what life should be. Is life really all about enjoyment, attainments and approvals? Right Principles are eternal treasures we are only permitted to carry with us beyond life. They are those values we leave for posterity sake. Any substance that does not benefit generations is not worth holding tenaciously. We cannot arrive at a destination we are not prepared to go. What we give time to, determines what we live behind for posterity sake. We could trace such trajectory from her first entanglement with wrong friends who she thought were friends but unknown to her are wolves in sheep's' clothing.

During the early days of her life, Princess had always loved to watch the flamboyant lifestyle of celebrities on movies, where they make a show of affluence and how that through their friends they could attain prominence earlier but unknown to her such are acts which do not depict the life's realities. Many celebrities have a successful public life but are private failures. They project temporal attainment without permanent values people could draw from as sources of inspiration. Many commit all their lives to chasing affluence without chasing respect. When we model our lives to what we see on media alone, we may not have a happy ending.

Oftentimes we are carried away by what we see on stages without truly examining the context on which it was done and the message passed through such acts. The message of a man begins from his life before his acts. We first become before we do and that is the major principle of great men. Many celebrities today do before they become and such act often leads to misery. They come to a time when they would discover that they are only taking a walk in life without having people who would wish to pattern after them. Sometimes such acts are embedded with lessons which we could see towards the end of such movies we see them feature in. We are often in a hurry to get carried away by the eloquence and flagrant show of affluence without picking the lessons.

Princess had always wanted to model her life after these celebrities she watched on movies. She sought to build her life in modeling career but never got a nod from her parents who insisted that she study professional course which would expose her to the world and hence her choice of History and International Relation. Princess did not know that all that glitters is not gold as many acts could portray. The Principle of choice is often seen as archaic in many homes but a child should be allowed to select what to become with the guidance of the parents and not to force them into what does not align with their talents and gifting.

Sometimes, Princess was tempted to practice what she saw from the home movies and when she is caught, she would cover up by using any means readily available. That was because what she gave her time and attention to, would always form her future. In the law of nature, what we constantly do, we become overtime. So what we give our time to, is not unconnected with what we see in us. Sometimes she would say, she was given a homework to do on a topic, which she could get the true essence of by watching some of those related topics on screen and because her parents were unaware of the needful from her course of study, they would quickly be swayed by such deceit. Princess would furnish her mind with such fantasies, bask in the euphoria of such fantasies at the detriment of her upbringing and that was not without a cost to pay for later. It will not be a bad idea to hang out once in a while to network and enjoy such events, but making it a habitual action is detrimental to a balanced growth. So we could understand the roots of her moral rot, which she never paid attention to until they became matters on the rise. Principles have been neglected so sharply that it almost looks so normal not observing them. Howbeit, some of these principles would make more sense bringing them out.

1. When a man does something morally wrong, that action not corrected could hamper the future. It took Princess much time to realize that those things she did not take care of at the beginning could obstruct further growth on her future pursuit. Many times we fail to watch our weaknesses as they grow until they become the monster that would hurt us tomorrow. When we do not match our actions with what we hope to have in future, we are on the high way to the rock. Such actions could be as a result of our inactions or a slide into activities not part of our moral upbringing like the case of Princess who became what he saw others do. Hardly do we often reflect on the effect of our negative responses to our environment, which would turn out to breed negativity influence. Most times, it could come

from people we empty our whole being to, who do not worth such trust. Trust is often a commitment of ones destiny to mere men. How we chose such men determines what we get out from it. To Princess, the choices were made out of emotion, which many are victims of today. They choose associations because they do not want to be slammed as being unfriendly. Such decisions often leave us at the mercy of those who see life as mere existence than living. When life is seen as existence, it is lived to fulfill emotions not realities. Princess lost the very essence of life when she began to see life as larger than its size, so it became so heavy for her to carry. When she began to look for helpers who would assist her in carrying and living her life, she did not know that emotion is life set on negative motion when not ruled by right sense.

1. Success is Preparation meeting opportunity regardless of time: A student was asked to define success and she said, "Success is when right opportunity collides with a prepared mind". Such

definition was the principle Princess neglected because she thought success was a product of luck. But that could not possibly resonate from what true success should be. Whatsoever luck gives a man will gradually deplete because accidental success is a monumental failure waiting to happen. We do not earn or inherit success; it is a work factor, which must tilt towards preparation and planning. When Princess was growing up, she had always loved successful people as she could be glued watching how men and women who have attained success flaunt affluence. Princess failed to realize that a good life is a product of hard work, commitment, right morals and character. Her Father often reminded her that the beauty of a man is in the size of his bank account while the beauty of a woman is her character, part of which is constant preparation. Time is not an enemy to a man of early preparation because any presumed waste of time, is perceived as a privilege of more time for preparation. A big task call for big planning and with such planning, success is a matter of when and not if. Many people today have failed not because it was in their nature to fail but because they have passed over opportunities repeatedly without knowing it. Opportunities are often subtle, they hid in the little things but men of discerning spirit will always pick it up when they see it. Many would have been millionaires but for lack of preparation. A child who does not learn the secret of hard work will engage in hard labor for people who have mastered the importance of preparation. All the time spent on partying by Princess, became obvious on the long run. Results are the products of examinations and that is how life functions. If there are no life examinations, promotion is far-fetched.

2. Destiny is not selective but preeminence is a product of preparation. Destiny is not selective because it differs and is peculiar with each person on earth. We are all destined to attain height but what you do to actualize such heights are completely up to you. There are no two individuals with the same destiny although the two individuals could be equal. The Parents of Princess were busy

preparing Princess without giving much attention to her brothers. These they did thinking that an investment on them would reduce the chances for Princess. They would treat her with all the love she ever needed and that was at the detriment of her brothers. These did not play well with her brothers who decided to allow fate decide their destinies. This goes against the African mindset where the male child is preferred to the female, since the heir apparent to every throne is the male. That has reduced the relevance of the female child but certainly not in this 21st century when the female children have proved wrong that ascertain that fortune only favors the male children. In the Stone Age, the female child is only good at procreation and good in the kitchen. They lived a slave kind of life, restricted from certain professions and skills exclusively reserved for the male folks. These made them redundant in creativity and relapse vital energies required for good work. But all these have seen the back of civilization especially now that women have exhumed high rate of dexterity and creativity, attaining highest proficiency at any given task. Well, the parents of Princess also think so, as the saying goes that a training of the female child is a training of the nation. But since Princess decided to choose another separate kind of life, preeminence must have its way. According to Aristotle, the great philosopher, *"all men are born equal"* and that suggests the fact that equality is the thing of the mind, hence a reflection at the decisions we make. Princess could have attained the height she had wanted to since there is no biasness in destiny. Everyone is born to accomplish a task and such task is reserved uniquely for each person. While it may not be the same, preeminence is a product of right preparation. What a person can do well is the reason such a person is sought after among equals. It is not a matter of doing the same thing but doing the same thing in a distinguished way is the hallmark of relevance. The quest for selection is not in destiny but in preeminence. In the University, many students study the same course and graduate with seemingly the same grade but premium is given to the person who can do best what everybody can do. This is not to say that effort made cannot be commended but we become authority at what we are flawless at doing. Many attend preeminence through consistency and others through hardship. To many people, preeminence could be through mentoring and all these are pointer to the pearl. If preeminence is attained through consistency, that means at one time, failure could be experienced. The fact that failure is experienced does not mean that attempt on the same project cannot be made. Princess failed to look at life from its true essence. That we make mistakes do not write off our ability to advance in the right cause. Men are infallible and as such, there should not be shame in failure but we must avoid remaining at the same level where we failed. Consistency means that something stronger could have halted our journey to relevance but against all odds, we fight to finish attaining victory and learning the requisite lessons expected of us. Fighting spirit is a winning spirit because it tends to keep us on our toes and help us activate tenacity. Consistency insists that the downfall of a man is not the end of his life but a change of position to reinforce for winning position. Princess believed that she had already been defeated and hence too late to fight, reclaiming her virtues. Character is not lost but can be changed. Secondly, others attained the level of preeminence through hardship. A gold, which does not pass through fire, cannot be appreciated in its beauty because the refining nature of gold is the long process it passed through fire. It must be long and the process must be enough for the lustrous nature to be seen. That means there is this kind of fire that comes through pressure that is necessary for attaining proficiency. If there is no fire, there may not be that igniting force to produce light. So light is ignited through fire no matter how small it may be. Many characters were refined at the corridor of hardship, bringing out the character of a man who through endurance allowed fire to produce its intent in him. In the search for pearls, fire helps in repositioning our priority and the understanding that gold is valued because of the process and time it passes through. Hardship sometime pushes us into diligence search for pearls of life to be able to avert poverty. The reason is because they confronted the challenges and finds a reason not to give up until they find solutions. *"Do not give up when it becomes tough"*, Princess' parent would always tell her because they know if such a principle is learnt on time, the ripple effect is always beneficial. As universal as time is for coordination, we often tend to abuse it. Many people give up almost the same time their breakthrough is due for celebrate. True living is a life lived sticking to time, knowing that the soothing balm of time is available for all who would insist on getting a testimony out of every challenge. But patience must have its way, if challenges must teach us the route to preeminence. It is also eminent upon our responsibility to speak up, when influence on us begins to suppress our survival. When a wrong message is assimilated for a long time, it ends up becoming the accepted message. This is true especially in recent times, when every source of information at our disposal is tilted towards discouraging us. Anything that cannot promote a better you and cannot be validated must be subjected to proper scrutiny. The price for preeminence begins with self-appraisal, for it is only when we pass the evaluation that we can focus on the real evil around us that belittles our optimal best. The questions that wise people ask are self-evaluation questions before they are coarse into doing anything. Having seen the place of consistence and learning through difficult times, which Princess neglected, Let us look at the place of mentoring in the next chapter, as it is quite exhaustive.

CHAPTER TEN

MENTORING NOT MINDED

What Princess never thought of was the place of mentoring; maybe she was not familiar with such word growing up. At every stage in the development of a child, there are things expected of such child and such expectations come with right knowledge and concept. Everyone would have thought that training also demands hard work, which parenting alone might not be enough. There is a time in the developmental stage of a child, where counselors and guidance are expected, to push forward what parenting could not attain. Many parents train their wards with emotional attachment and as such they are not able to apply both wisdom and corrective rods to align their wards in the right direction. Oftentimes, the child could feel hated when rebuked by the parents and hence the need for mentoring from a trusted guidance and counselor.

Mentoring has been the super ingredient lacking in child's upbringing in Africa and if there are, the right ones are very scarce. The problem of Africa is hinged on this space, where there are not enough trusted hands to fall into when shaping our choices and aspirations. Mentoring is giving value away for free with the intent that the free gift becomes a place value to the receiver. It is training for the right preparation into the real world which school has not done. Such real world requires right preparation from people who are truthful and sincere. It is a state of apprenticeship where the lower is upgraded to an aspired height of the higher force and beyond.

Mentoring is not dependent on age and can never be attributable to such factor as a yardstick. Many have wondered why it is often so neglected in Africa especially in the 21st century. The reason is not far from the realities of entitlement mentality ravaging the century especially among the youths of Africa, where they assume anything they wanted is their right of entitlement. And if they do not get what they want, they believe they are neglected. They never worked for what they deserved and if they ever did, they want to arrive immediately after they begin. There is a process to everything and also secrets to anything in life. Only the wise are able to patiently wait to get it. They never realized that for anything one needs, such a person must work it out by being relevant and also staying relevant. They sincerely need what they are not willing and ready to offer and since they are not willing to offer such as they need, they think getting it is part of their inheritance. There has never been any valuable received that was not first strategically given upon right positioning. It may not be in the same measure as expected but what is given should be of great impact before it can make meaning out of life. The truth of the matter is that for anything ever imagined, there are people who have attained authority level on the same part before now. If princess had been handed over to a mentor on time, maybe the wrong part followed would have been averted but rather wrong peers, who also never had the opportunity to be mentored were allowed to influence her.

We must come to a level even in the curriculum of our higher educations, where the aspect of mentoring is made compulsory for all students; maybe it could also start from the basic education. In mentoring, we are able to identify our weaknesses, since mistakes are allowed so that we could be better corrected through our mentors before it becomes a monumental shame outside. Mentoring should be seen as a two-way traffic, it is demanding as well as demands. Many have thought it is only dependent on the giver, but the receiver must also be willing to receive before it becomes effective. When something is given and it is received, it does not generate any positive impact.

To the mentor, there are basic things expected of such person among which are faithfulness to be committed to the task and trust to be disciplined. I have pulled out two important concepts; faithfulness and commitment. These two things are independent of each other for a mentor who had accepted the responsibility to mentor a person. Many mentors are faithful but not committed and trusted. Trust is a like a bank draft, it must be signed before it can be used. Responsibility must be given before it is expected and likewise commitment. If time is committed, the reward may come in as financial. Trust must also be sued for since it may involve confidential information availed to the mentor for effective mentoring.

The mentee is not left out in the things expected of such, which includes obedience, commitment and respect. Africa expresses such virtues but it is pertinent to note that such virtues are gradually eroding. That is because such values are not eschewed as the only policy and since it is not the only policy for all, many tend to follow that which is more convenient for them. This may be the reason why there is not effective mentoring in the 21st century. Many see success as a sole responsibility of a man irrespective of how it is gotten but lasting success requires character to be maintained. People who got to the top without being well mentored may not last at the position, if they were not taught the principle to remaining at the top. There are certain laws of aerodynamics, which also play out in human attainments and pursuits. According to Isaac Newton, *a body will remain at the state of rest or if in motion, remain same until acted upon by an external force.* There are certain principles, which must be eschewed to be able to maintain the top. So consistency, hardship and mentoring are gateway to preeminence.

CHAPTER ELEVEN
THE MENTAL METAL

If there was something Princess lack that was obvious, it is her inability to pay attention to her mental strength. This has something to do with her wholeness, being so beautiful a Princess should have depicted a total package comprising of physical, mental, moral and intellectual beauty. The things known as the basic ingredients are missing in her. Ingredients are so called because they are the basic requirements necessary for capacity generation and successful life.

Many, like Princess often pay less attention to this aspect of wholeness and that plays out on the long run in the future they see. Princess was so much carried away by her beauty that she believed nothing else is as important as physical beauty. She later discovered that what she had done to herself by not paying attention to her whole life is more damaging to her self-worth.

Wholeness is attained when an attention is given to all aspects of life, which holistically looks at spiritual, moral, physical and mental life. To Princess, all that matters to her was her body and physical appearance even if it was on an empty head. A beautiful girl with an empty head is a disaster waiting to occur and the effect is always colossal. When the grey hair of a man is devoid of wisdom, then the grey hairs becomes a mockery to all.

"Beautiful people don't lack anything", was often the general believe to many people. Rarely do must aspiring leaders pay utmost attention to other sides of life like mental training. What then are the basic ingredients needed for a holistic life? Are there truly other things needed in the quest for a fulfilled and all round successful life? Above all things needed for a fulfilled life,

is a good mental attitude. These are attitudinal in nature and often hidden from the sight of people but surely, it is of a necessity.

The word mental is connected to the mind and since the mind is a vital tool so long as Human is concern, it must be properly guided. It plays out through a heart of gratitude to the things received and to the things expected. This habit is a sign of good mental strength because when the mind sees things on a positive note, it triggers gratitude. We cannot truly give when we are not totally sold out to sound mind. In being grateful, we understand that we are totally not in control of what life offers although some offers can be under our control. Princess was not always in the habit of being grateful for things received which made her parents always wonder at the things that come her way. She often does not think that it is courtesy to be grateful. Favor comes to people who see every gift as a privileged not a right. It may not play out on big things but in those little things, which we often seem to neglect. It is normal to reciprocate such attitude of appreciation through giving more. We often complain about everything we get and that hinders more rewards from coming our way. Through the attitude of gratitude, we open up for more piles of goodwill in our lives.

We must also learn to feel our feelings and not being in the habit of bottling up our emotions. Many people often live to please others even when it hurts most. They prefer to appear real with fake identity and as such they end up living to please others. We are first called to please who we are called to be before we become who we are made to be. We may not always feel the same way, which is what makes us unique individually and we must show our individual uniqueness in our daily actions. It is good to be angry and it is also good to be happy, all must be displayed in measures to what is expected. The problem with feelings is that it has to a large extent dictated the way many live. We are not to make major decisions anchoring on our emotions. Emotions are not the best state to help us fathom our decisions as our environment could influence our emotions. In showing forth our feelings, we must be sure not to allow the cancer of resentment to erode us away from the pursuit for relevance. Many resent not because they would assume the state of the person whom they resented but just to show off superiority. When we do not see anything good in others around us, we may be blinded to see the strength that makes us unique as individuals. Princess would always look down on the people who she judged lower than her class and that made her not to have enough network and bond with others who would have helped her out after school. The truth about life is that many whom we resent on our way up, may hinder us from attaining our aspired position because they may be the ladders to the next level we aspire to assume. This has often been a stumbling block to many people today, limiting them and the people who would have directly benefitted from them. There is no competition that we are enlisted in life but for self-development, which we must be jealously doing. Life does not consist in the abundance of things seen around us but what is made from the little we have achieved. Resentment will always breed self-pity, where we begin to see more of our weakness than our strengths. Such could inhibit our growth in life because we invest our time on looking at those things, which we could have attained, that became a mirage. Men who ever achieved relevance, never dwelt more on their past rather they focused on the future which is very vital. Self-pity could result to comparison and blame game.

The cankerworm called 'blame washing' is ravaging so many people today, where many often shift blame because they just believe they cannot be wrong. This is a serious stumbling block in life today. The first sign of failure is not being bold and courageous enough to accept our wrongs but instead look for someone to pass the blame to. The fact that we accept our wrongs is the bravest thing to do. We must understand that we are in control of our attitudes and emotions and hence must not allow people to run them for us. Our emotions must not affect our decisions if the giant in us must roar. We provoke the good things of life through a good mental attitude. The hallmark of leadership in every field of human endeavor is maintaining a right attitude about life and that would yield a positive result, which academic certificates may not provide us with. The center of every pursuit is on these ingredients and people cannot give you trust until they can trust what you do.

Many people who are stranded today are not because they are cursed as they supposed but because they failed to yield these fruits, which position people on their aspired destinations. There are habits that we must not give in to for a healthy mental attitude. These are addictions to alcohol and pornography, which could lead to metal retardation and impair our height of reasoning and mental articulation. Many are victims of such unhealthy habits and that have destroyed their potentials. If all we could do is to live up to these expectations, our world will be that which we create to suit our personality.

CHAPTER TWELVE

VISION: THE CONQUERING POWER

The vision of a man has remained the power against every division and has opened him up to a limitless provision. The power to become is in the understanding of vision. The power of right attitude and character has remained the most influential power, with which many have recreated their world. Suffice it to say that the limit a man could go is the limit his vision can carry him. Princess was surrounded with aids and helps but it takes maintaining a position to remain in the same position. How addicted a man is to vision determines his addition to the world. The reason is because the vicinity where right attitude is found is the same place the visitation of a man is seen. The sun cannot rise at the same place where it sets and to expect more is certainly to do more. To whom much is given, work is given to prove the trust reposed on such a person. Nothing activates favor more than a vision driven man who has built a reputable character. To be stagnated in life is to live a visionless lifestyle. Relevance begins when we understand the demand for living a fulfilled life which vision is a major non-negotiable requirement. Nothing in life can be addressed if it cannot be arrested. What we give attention to determine what give us profit. Princess began to give attention to things not propelled by right vision and it lived to wait for her in future until something drastic is done to avert negative consequences.

The beauty of life is the just recompense it gives back based on what is being put into it. Nothing done in secret is permanent because attitude cannot be hidden for long. What has been made visible by the realities of light cannot be hidden from men. Light, no matter how dim it seems to appear cannot be used as an instrumental tool to propagate darkness and dark dealings. What is made obvious is the basis for passing judgment because nothing can be judged until it can be seen. What a man gets in life is the accumulation of his attitude to life. Nothing can be birthed until something is felt because it takes travail to bring forth a child. Likewise, vision is birthed after a travail for the right attitudes to life is done. The womb is the beauty of a woman as vision is the beauty of a man who aspires relevance in time and eternity. The travail of a woman can be better appreciated when we hunger for what we cannot visualize or things we have no immediate control over. Each time we make reference to a fulfilled life, vision is checked but each time pains are to be measure, the travail of a woman is considered. Princess never took into account the requirements that are necessary for what she had aspired to become, maybe the cost was unknown to her at the beginning.

What is not known at the beginning may not be appreciated at the end. Perhaps no body was able to point her to the right direction and what the demands are for a successful life, hence a mentor was lacking in her life.

Greatness is not an overnight achievement but it is the ability to see the painful end with the rigorous process and being willing to pass through it. Vision preserves purpose and energizes a man to press forward to the mark of high calling. People who quit on the way as a result of painful strive are not likely to be candidates of success but those who by nature of use when vision is involved have learnt to lead their generation and eventually win indeed.

Lack of vision is why many are still stranded today like Princess, who had academic certificate she was not trained in character to use. They parade with qualifications, which are not applied to solving the yearnings and aspirations of people. As long as the needs of people are not met, life remains a mirage to a visionless person. In life, the best approach to learning is to know what people have learnt to get to the position we aspire to attain. As such we master the approaches they used to attain their visions and the provisions needed to attain such height. When the secrets of people are known, the tendencies of making the same mistakes they made are minimized. That way, vital energy is channeled to productivity and that unleashes our potentials with such a navigational compass called vision.

The projections of life is anchored on the analytical study on vision and the direction it tends to show and that can only be realistic to a man who had written down such visions as he journeys in life. Wisdom is needed in the application of vision to determine when, where and how questions of life. Wisdom is a call that is answered by people who have studied from the experiences of others and not by the experiences their mistakes have taught them. Wisdom is made manifest by her seeds. The pain of travail in birthing a vision is the greatest pain in life anyone could experience and that could be likened to the pain of childbirth every woman goes through. If Princess had known she would have planned better in her life. But she had another opportunity to right her wrong and that process was not triggered until she met her childhood friend called Rose. Second chance is never a right but a privilege, which we may not be entitled to all times, and hence the need to value what was once handed down to us by utilizing second chance very well. We may not truly appreciate a second option as we would for the first choice until we see it pass by swiftly. We are not expected to abuse the first opportunity to pattern our lives to the visions of our calling. The pain of vision lingers for as long as it is still inside of us but when birthed the joy of knowing what it could do in us is enough to cushion the effect of such pains. The joy of education is when we eventually become relevant in the society, without which the essence is defeated. The pains to birth vision could be discouraging to the bearer but the joy of success is a consolation. The products a man expect from his farm, is the joy for working hard in the planting session. Vision does not make the carrier to be ashamed nor afraid of what the future holds. A man of vision cannot be stranded in life because even when he is disarmed, bouncing back is a matter of when, not if. It does not take note of timing because it must speak at the end. No person ever attracts help until people know the driving force behind what the person does.

CHAPTER THIRTEEN

THE MAGIC

Princess thought to give life a magical approach with the intention of getting a mystical result but life does not work in such a way. We cannot expect what we did not commit into sowing in our approach to life. The fact that every success in life has secrets makes life less magical. Nothing is truly known until we are able to decode the pattern thereof. There is a code to success and without unlocking such code; it is practically impossible to access success.

Every room that stores a precious pearl is always secured and almost very difficult to be accessed by all. It is an utter frustration to be around the corridor of a house without having access to the key of the house. A man can occupy a house without having access to such house because he has restricted entry into the house. Many like Princess are occupying a space without having access to the environment. That is in reality how it is when we attempt to search for a pearl without knowing the secret to accessing it. The reason why few people enjoy what others lack is because of what they know. Such knowledge if not decoded cannot be beneficial to all. Everything possible may not be available to a man who does not know how to decode the secret to the pearls of life. The first step towards getting what we want in life is to truly know what we want. Many people are stranded today because what they need is unknown to them and because they do not know, they will not know what to do to get what they need.

Princess was stranded after school because she is not aware of what she truly needs to do to get what she had aspired to become. It is as frustrating, as it is to a man who is in search for the unknown and not knowing the right direction on how to get what he wants. The difference between getting the pearl and searching for the pearl is direction. Two people may arrive at the same destination at the same time when they have the right direction or they may arrive at different time, when they have different directions. It is also possible that they may wander around on the road when they both have no direction. Many are webbed in the mire of darkness and utter frustration today for lack of direction.

Life is easy when the light of direction reflects on our part to destiny and the difference is the revelation of the secret to knowing what to do at all times. We get stranded on the road we are unaware of but through direction, we live a life of vision through the illuminating power of direction. What we do not know exist cannot be changed by us. Princess needed an illumination to attract success and only the power of knowledge could do, which is the knowledge of the right direction.

Many people want the best out of life; best of Children, career, relationship, work but the price to getting it; they have no idea of or the cost. Every attractive and priceless pearl has a price tag because what is attractive is expensive. The best life is lived when we find the best approach to life. Not all keys can open a particular door hence the right key must be applied. The right definition to frustration is looking for a way in a seemingly no way. The right place for preparation is in the secret place, which is more on the inside, and the result is found outside when it comes, which is the outcome of right dreams and clear cut vision. The things, which are seen often, are paid for from what is not seen because what is seen is temporal and what is not seen is eternal. That is why it was said earlier that character is the true beauty of a woman. A woman who neglects it for other things may end up using other things to maintain the cost of not having the right character.

A solid building depends on the right foundation laid. If the foundation of eternal value were not solidly laid, what attracted people to a man would soon fade away when the winds of life bellow. The values of a man are deliberately built and it comes with a price tag. Princess would have decided to maintain her values while she was growing up, without allowing negative influence from her environment but she decided to ignore right values. The beauty of character is not the action taken but a decision to build right character is the first step to the unveiling of the beauty. It is first decided in the heart before it is played out in the actions we take. The heart is the site for influence and must be protected from wrong influence around us since the issues of life comes from it.

The issues of life either bring success or failure. Whatever that is received is traceable to the imaginations of the heart. A woman who failed in life, failed from the heart before failing in life. A woman of dreams is a standard for others both to will and to do, which is reflected in the script her life plays out. Many in the search for a pearl have embraced so many things in other to appeal to people because they believe that the life of a man consists in the abundance of the possessions he has. The honey in a comb is not dependent on the comb but the combination of the right substances to produce the honey. A fish is conditioned to live inside water and so it does. That is because the fish has identified its natural inhabitant based on the character of the fish. No fish survives outside water likewise nobody survives outside the values they have identified with. We attract respect when people could see in us what they cannot see in the environment we live in. When the sayings of a man are consistent, his actions would be the same.

The standard we build through the values we set for our living, determines how we are seen. Gold is celebrated among stones because of its quality and the process it undergoes to reflect true beauty and that is why it is sought for all over the world. Anything that is readily available is not totally valuable even when it may be easily accessible. If we must maintain relevance in the sight of people, we must as a matter of importance retain in us the scarce virtues in our environment. Such values, which are very rare, are the reason many are sought for and celebrated. The evidence of beauty is not in the physical appearance but in the attitude we depict when we fight the battles of the soul, which is equally the battles of life. To believe what is new, we must seek for what is true and only then will our freedom be secured. The difference between attitude and altitude is right values for life. We actually are the product of what we allow inside of us and what we allow inside us reflects on things we do, say or see. We act differently when we think differently and that depends on what we allow to form in our heart. We are accepted when the concept we project is different from what the environment have seen for a long time that has been accepted as the best. So long as gold remains in its raw form, it does not differ from other stones but when it passes through a refining process, its value is visible and enhanced. The true beauty is not what is seen outwardly because what retains attention is the intention not perceived as usual by all. Let us then look at the errors under the sun.

CHAPTER FOURTEEN
THE ERRORS

Certain things people experience in life is as a result of what they did or what they did not do. It is either the error of omission, which is the error of not doing the things they are expected to do or the error of commission, which implies doing what should not be done. Men are only in control of what they are yet to do, certainly not what they have already done. There are two errors under the sun, which have truncated many destinies. These two errors are:

The Error of doing it because people do it

This error is also known as the error of following the norm because it appears fashionable. In life, we are either a product of what people sowed into us or what we sowed into ourselves. What we sowed into ourselves can be as a result of the things we allowed access into our lives and what people sowed into us, could be as a result of the associations we keep. We often do things because we think everyone does it. That everyone does something does not portray it as being right. Among the few choices we are allowed to make in life is the choice of who we give our time and treasures and our talents, which reflect in the things we do. These three important gifts are in our control to decide how they are being managed. While many choose to control their life on earth through these aspects, some have modeled their lives by being careful whom they give these vital treasures for destiny sake. To Princess, this decision was not well managed and hence the influence on her impaired her aspirations and ambitions in life while she was growing up. Many highfliers have crashed through the error of doing things because people did it.

The best way to the top is self-brainwashing to believe that there is nobody with bad character who ever remained at the top even if such a person gets to the top. To be brainwashed by someone is to believe that the only way to the top is through the wrong route.

Evil association is an enemy to good morals. What we spend our time on determines what we get out of life. A man who spends much time in the loop will always carry the bad odor that comes from defecates. Association is the fastest way to predict and decide the future of a man. The character of a man is controlled through influence and who we repeatedly study about, is whom we become overtime. When an eagle spends much time with a duck, it learns to live on the land. We cannot grow above the environment we subject ourselves. The character of a man is either acquired or learn and that is why genes and environment play all important role is the building and formation of a man. The illuminating power of the light is only seen in darkness. It sometimes appear easier to learn evil than good because whatever has no value, does not take much time and effort to master. That is the reason why the processing time for pearls are different from ordinary stones. When a person is subjected into a specific environment, it does not need force to conform into such environment. Every student graduates to become what has been taught in the class and what he has repeatedly received. The power of association is very strong and can hinder the power of self-will. Princess was having a good time with the wrong people and it robbed off on the person she turned to become. We first learn how to do a task before we perfect on it. This perfection is a product of overtime practice and when practice is consistent overtime, it becomes our character. That is the reason why many that were nurtured with good morals suddenly become worse than anticipated. There is always a need for right people around us, as part of the right choices we should make in life to be able to fulfill purpose.

The difference between what parents can do and what the children can do, is a matter of time. The same action and steps taken will result to the same manifestation in a matter of time.

Evidence of good training is seen through the actions displayed not in the talks. The best way to model an individual is to do what you want the person to do more than the things you said should be done. As they keep seeing it done, they learn how best to do it. That is why example is always the best way to teach. Many who desire to grow have often think that growth is difficult and since they perceived growth as being difficult, they resolved to remain at the same spot for long. Children do not often do what their parent said but what they see them do. Could that have been the case of Princess? Not until we understood whom she learnt from growing up. We saw the media training, which she was exposed to and she began to pattern after the models she saw since that was the true representation of the person she had always wished to become. The constant exposure to the negative aspect of the media led her to a negative influence. Many African Parents are not in control of what their Children watch, who they extend their hands of friendship and how they behave in the presence of their Children. Overtime, the result is often out of control as a result of carless lifestyle of many parents and guidance. An African adage says *"a man, who fetches ant-infested firewood, should be ready for a contention with the lizard"*. Where a man gets authority is the place he spends time in because in the search for knowledge, remaining in such corridor of authority for a long time will result to retaining enough knowledge to wade off ignorance. Where there is no plan to acquire knowledge, the search for knowledgc remains irrelevant since part of what we get in life is through influence people have on us. In life, we would discover through careful observation that 50% of what we know are what we were taught, 30% we discover and 20% are through impact books and tapes had on us. This may be otherwise for some persons but the influence of people on us have strong impact on how our lives play out. To wade off societal vices ravaging this generation and the coming generations, parental influence must supersede the media influence on the rising generation. A deliberate effort must be committed towards the upbringing of Children. When such effort is effectively committed, the society will be better for it. The womb that brought forth Children must be committed to protecting them. The life of Princess as we noted was not in the control of her parents, who were weak at discharging their function using the rod and the staff. The rod must not be spared and the staff must not be far from reach to be able to draw in love. The combination of these two important instruments would have been necessary to point Princess on the road to success without much stumbling blocks in her quest for the pearl. Princess wanted what she was not willing to pay for and then could not eventually access it. Greatness has a price tag and to become great is to pay the prize for greatness.

Princess was a herald of new era of rest at least that was only fair to be expected having been lavishly spent on by her parents. She was seen as a new chapter of blessing and favor to come since her realm was to produce a reign of rest and peace. Her parents had promised to see to the realization of her dreams and aspirations. Princess was beautifully adored at least there was nothing she lacked and hence became the envy of her mates. Men lost their breaths for a second at the sight of her beauty. When greatness is within, it could silence physical appearance and minimize its loudness. That goes on to show that there was nothing nature gave that could sustain greatness when there is bankruptcy of good attitude. Life often proffers us with choices but the choice we make decides our lives. All we need in life is fully embedded in the choices we make. One seed of greatness in us has generations in mind and that should guild the choice of association we keep. Such choices earlier made are the foundation upon which we build our destinies.

The Lack of Self-Control

This is another error, a web many people are often caught in. One of the hardest battles in life is the battle of the mind, the ability to subject our minds under control. We often have control over other things we think are important needs of life. For instance, the control for power, family, wealth, job and religion are often the places many exert control over without the mastery of self. And because they do not learn the art of self-control, they loss every other thing they have struggled for in life. It is like a car, we truly cannot control it until we have mastered the use of the steering. The avowed assumption that self-control is the hardest thing anyone can do, is quite synonymous to the statement that *what we give attention in life does not necessarily matter so long as results are obtained.*

A farm that is not given the necessary attention through tending will be under the attack of weeds. Self- control is a deliberate effort and it demands a decision to maintain. The body is the eye of the mind and how clean our mind is can be traceable to the things our mind ponders over and things our body yearns for. Princess never hallowed her body but rather decided to allow her emotions rule over her conscience and right morals, the results of which became so unbearable to her. She was an example of a desperado who would rather use anything to get what she wants even if it involves the use of her body since she was well endowed. She has all her days dreamt of having a blissful future but never had the will power to work out her relevance through self-control. She perhaps could be an example for many people who crave for fame more than anything else and are willing to do anything to actualize their desperation. She must have noted the weaknesses of her parent to tame her and then decided to pattern after her immediate environment to meet up with the current demands for the now. Such demands anchored on the principle of using what one has to get what the needs are. When careless lifestyle begins to play the tune of our dance steps, regrets come knocking at the end.

The failure of every man comes through an uncontrolled obvious weakness, which may not matter much in the beginning but is capable of destroying the seed of greatness in us. Anything that is capable of destroying the seed of greatness is no doubt the worst enemy to any man. It may not look like a threat at first but if not tamed, could hinder access to the treasures of life. The obvious weakness of Princess was her uncontrolled self and that did not go well with her. When a problem is well understood, it is half way solved.

Every uncontrolled self could lead to severe consequences. As it is to the laws of any nation, so it is to the human laws.

Human laws are given to govern a nation and avoid excesses that may have severe consequences in the future. The need for law is to regulate activities of men that may affect the environment.

Every Nation has a formal constitution, principles or laws that help to direct the government for effective governance. There is the principle of cause and effect put in place by the law, to forestall breakdown of law and order. This also plays out at the things we do and the cost we pay to accessing the pearl. There is no citizen who is above the law of a land and that also suggests similarly that nobody will grow above the principles of life. These principles are the guiding factor towards the things we get out of life. The actions and inactions of life are necessary to avoid the pitfalls of life. The best or the worst things of life we get are totally dependent on our self-control. Across the world today are people who expose themselves to many social vices and bad attitude is as a result of lack of self-control, discipline and focused life. Love compels us to live a self-controlled life, when we build it as a character. The power of choice is the voice that speaks louder and it could also influence more of our decisions. Such choices may be necessitated by the understanding of the life we have. Such understanding is the fact that life is a replication of what we allow into our heart. It may not reflect almost immediately but must surely speak at the end and not lie. The only thing that is wrong with being virtuous is our decision not to be virtuous. Princess decided to go for a temporal enjoyment at the expense of her future and the end result brought shame to her. People around may not have seen it but they may have said it to her, the dangers of such lifestyle.

Princess could only stop people from saying what they saw but certainly cannot stop them from seeing the results of her decisions and since it is seen, the sayings cannot be stopped.

When we learn to talk to our minds, we are able to control our bodies and what we allow to happen to it. Virtuousness is the ability to subject self under control. Many have mastered the act of controlling the family, business, wealth and nations but have not learnt how to control self. They constantly speak and act to show total weakness at self-control. To measure the greatness of a man, we must first study the level of self-control such man has developed because great men respond not to detects of their body but the content of their character. Princess loved pleasures of life just as many people want to arrive early at a destination they never prepared for.

CHAPTER FIFTEEN

THE LIGHT OF CONDUCT

The actions of any man are the incubated words not spoken. It is like bottling up words until it is opened by situations either favorable or unfavorable. We cannot truly know the true character of a man until such a man is subjected to situations he is not attuned to. A man will always arrive at his destination when he follows the right route. There is no man who succeeds accidentally and even when such is said to occur, only time will show how unprepared such a person was in order to maintain such success. Nothing said is truly relevant until there is a reflection of such words through a corresponding action. There is no victory in view when there is no action invested to expect such a result. Having the right knowledge necessitates doing the right thing and the effect is seen through the results that are produced. We may never be noticed, when we only depend on spoken words but through what we commit to doing. Some people are known to do more and say less but even at the little said, the abundance of the heart can be ascertained. What we become is replications of what we have consistently done. We do not make reference to words spoken more than we do to actions taken in life by a man. If the actions are taken based on the right intentions then the words said will be righty used. When a man learns to speak the right words, he attracts the right actions from his environment and for the future. The future responds to the right button only the right words could press. The creative ability is in our mouth, which we may not know until we begin to act rightly. The authority we are entrusted with is as a result of the responsibilities we are able to handle well by committing ourselves to doing things right. When an action is propelled through the purity of the heart, the effect is positive and the result rewarding. Nothing is truly made manifest until something is acted upon. It could be through an instruction given or through information received. Our actions must not be done with emotional attachment in order to avoid reprisal effects of regrets. We must learn to respond to instructions with the heart to enable us to learn and respond to information with the intention to add to our knowledge. All the information we receive must first be evaluated to know the purpose so as to be able to deploy it well. Actions are like bridges that link spoken words with results. Humans are made speaking spirit and they are wired to create with words and what they say, they could create so as to see it. In the search for the pearls of life, we must understand the importance of right speaking. Words are very powerful as tools for creativity. The strength of any man is known through the words he speaks. The physical appearance of any man does not show the true nature of the man because words are the identity of a man. As a matter of fact, outward adornment with gold apparels can be deceptive because it can only cover the nature that may have a rotten character. So every package must be duly evaluated before taken home to avoid regrets in life. Whosoever saw Princess would certainly admire her curves but not until you unveil the person behind the veil. Certainly there are many people today who parade themselves with rotten attitudes like Princess, which do not show at the way they are packaged in appearance. The inner beauty is the grace of the outward beauty that projects people into favor with men. Many people spend time on the outward appearance and then little or no time developing the inner man (Character). In the search for the pearls of life, the inner beauty is the magnet that is use to attract such pearls. The inner beauty requires some basic ingredients, which must be balanced. One of the ingredients is the appetite for sound knowledge. The adage goes that *he who does not know and does not wish to know cannot be trusted to know what the future holds*. Learning must be a deliberate and consistent effort. Any man who desires to access the pearl must learn to study until enough light is shunned around him because knowledge is light. Such light is capable of creating a bright future even in seemingly scarce resources. One of the pursuits of men is appetite for knowledge, which is capable of producing light. Such light cannot be hidden when it radiates. Another way inner beauty is maintained is through a guide to what we allow into our mind. The mind is the center of thoughts and thus must be guided properly through the things we allow into it. The role of media today must be duly stated and we must be sincere to check what we allow into our lives through what we hear and see. It takes discipline to guide the gates of our heart against things capable to distorting it. It is always a daunting task especially in the modern world where we are almost not in control of what we hear and see. The environment decides on what it wants us to see and what it wants us to hear due to lack of regulations on what is allowed to fly into our surroundings. Our actions are gradually tilting towards what the environment wants and a deviation from that takes much struggle if not almost impossible. A child grows up, with the conditioning of the environment and hence it makes parenting a very herculean task as the battle for morals are left at the mercy of the environment. This ought not to be so when discipline is first instilled in every person from beginning and the right patterning carried on. The task of guiding our hearts must be a task we are not willing to mortgage for anything on earth. Our knowledge must grow above the distractions of the world and as such, we tend to get more focused on the things that would enable us get access to the pearls of life. Only then can we truly say we have successfully navigated through the winds of evil and the ever-increasing distractions in our environment.

Right conducts must be the attitude of any wise person who is in search for the pearls of life. Self-development must be from inside with the result seen on the outside. No matter how hidden a mouth odor may appear, it is only hidden from a person who is far away. The deception of words can only last as long as there is no right platform to show it. Without the inner beauty, accepting instructions and corrections become very difficult especially when it comes from a more experienced person. People who have no respect for right conducts have no value for tangible things. They are always agog with things of no value and essence. We cannot truly give value when we do not appreciate things of utmost value. There is always a reward for every right attitude displayed. People who consciously live right attract right things of life. No man ever goes far more than his attitude about life. Unity of the spirit, sympathy, love, a tender heart, a humble spirit are all the products of right conduct and these are the requirements for a successful life. Princess needs more of these conducts in her daily living to gain more in her search for the pearls of life.

CHAPTER SIXTEEN

PRINCESS AND HER REALITIES

There is this mindset that love could gain us the good things of life but the realities outside the academic world has thought us otherwise. One would have thought that the love we garner on campus could translate into fortunes of life but this is not true for a life outside school. People could love so much as to avail you of their time and treasure but when it comes to doing the real job, it is competent driven and he who can do the job is same who gets the job. Princess was loved from her home and everything was given to her on a platter of gold at least those things, which are readily available and affordable to her parents. When she got admission, with her amazing curves, many were attracted to her to have a bit of that natural endowment she possessed but that is not without a cost. If they cannot get a feel of it, a touch could do, with such mindset, many gave her anything just to lure her to offer her smiles. But like every other woman, her natural endowments were often her greatest bargaining power and any manly man could do anything to get. Men, like flies will always be attracted in the direction of any aroma they like. They could give out anything to align with their emotional swift. These realities became a mirage when Princess discovered that love alone does not offer the good things of life.

21st century is the era of white-collar job and that was what everyone considers as a favorable end, especially those who are privileged to see the four walls of the higher institutions. The quest for a good life is perceived to begin from getting employed in an air-conditioned fitted office. That was because the continent of Africa is yet to scale out our prospects, which is often displayed through our can-do spirit.

The mission of Princess was thwarted when she realized that the realities outside school is anchored on the value we could contribute to the solution-thirsty world. The place of white-collar job is gradually eroding, with an ever-increasing scarcity of jobs and the need for qualified individuals who have both the character and aptitude to occupy such offices. Like Princess who failed to take into account her character and prepare for raining days, the chances are quite sleek for unprepared graduates since the competition is quite intense after graduation.

There are differences between what we think we can do and what we can actually do in the real sense. What we think we can do may be as a result of the academic certificates we have acquired not having the required experiences to back it up. It could also be as a result of what we are told either to make us feel good or to make us settle at the lowest ebb of life. For Princess, her pride was anchored on her natural endowments only, which she exalted above her real personality. What we can truly do is geared towards our preparation, a deliberate building of the right character and our aptitude learned to be distinguished among our equals. It is at this stage that love translates to substance which is truly valued to enable us attract relevance. We all may not be academic maggots, which are ever digging for increased knowledge but the capacity to develop is wrapped in our character towards facing the realities of life. To say that success can only be defined when we acquire academic certificate is to relegate to the background the importance of developing our skills and talents. All the time Princess was searching for relevance, there was no attention given to train her in entrepreneurial skills, which would have helped her after school. Many have silenced their skills because they could not get their supposed dream jobs but unknown to them, love alone does not guarantee access to that dream job People could love you enough to recommend you for a job but it would take more than a recommendation to keep the job going. When realities dawned on Princess, she began to seek for just another route to close up the gap she could not measure up with, but that would cause her much.

One day she was so depressed unto death and while she was wondering on what next to do, she ran into one of her lecturers who was also one of her secret admirers while she was in school. She could not hide her feelings anyone because it was obviously telling on her that all was not well with her.

"Hello Princess! How has life been with you? He asked with a straight look at her, only imagining again her curves but this time, looking at the Princess who was not in such a mood. Princess, who was not too concerned with the looks of the man

opened up to him about her frustrations since graduation and her inability to realize her age-longed dreams and aspirations. *"It was not too good"*, replied Princess to which a little discussion broke out between them. He began to tell her how she could believe in herself, deploy her skills and talent into wealth creation by understanding how dreams could be achieved. A little discussion that never lasted long but that was a little relieve on Princess at that moment. That was a pointer that a savior is required to guild Princess on the right cause.

CHAPTER SEVENTEEN

THE SAVIOR

It is certainly not the size of a champion that crowns her but the heart with which she sees herself. It is also not the size of a crown that validates a queen but the size of her dreams. There is nothing easy on the surface of the earth but men make things as easy as they would want it to be. We do not see a warrior at the battlefield but what she does behind the scene that crowns her a warrior. Princess would have thought that there are no solutions to her plight but that is only as long as she judges her end from her present state. Something could still be done but until it is done, nothing is seen. A hero is not known at his slumber but when he stands. When we see an environment secured by a lion, we see an environment ruled by a warrior.

A warrior is known by the courage with which he wades off challenges. The quest for the pearl is a quest embarked upon with determination pressing towards the mark and not likely to give up on such quest. There is a sleeping Lion in the heart of every brave Champion that could be quickened by someone in form of a Savior. Such a Savior may not necessarily be human but could also be circumstances and surroundings, which could put a man on his foot and get him brace up to challenges. Princess was not aware of what awaits her because there was no enough effort put to pull out the giant within.

Rose was a childhood friend of Princess whose principles project more than her personality. When it gets tough in life, only the men with the right principles become principals. When the principles of a man are clear and unalloyed, it is only a matter of time and his personality will be celebrated. When the principles

Princess had learnt became blurred as a result of negative influence, her personality became questionable and only the right Principles could help her. That principle was found in Rose, who had ascended the position of a director in a big multinational firm. What a man holds on determines what people would hold him for. We cannot compromise our principles for our personality because what promotes our personality is our works not our talks. We see much talks today and not too many works and as long as our works are not clear, our personality cannot be truly celebrated.

Oftentimes, we experience things and see people who wish to be known by what people say and not what people saw they did. When people can see the same thing we say we are, they say us differently. Lions are very calculative; they know how to attack and when to attack without missing. That is a notable fact about Champions too and like Rose, they know and feel the pulse of others for early intervention. To touch lives, we must be willing to spread our tentacles wide and extend beyond our boundaries. Only then can we truly reach out to create influence exactly what Rose did to Princess. But this must be viewed both sides because to be acknowledged, we must advance forward and act in the right direction. There have not been anything attained without required actions.

The truth of the matter is that what we do not fight for, we cannot touch and if we cannot touch it, we cannot also keep it. To this end, Princess must break the cradle of prison pipcline, which has prevented her from seeing the long awaited light at the end of the tunnel to salvage her future and defend the future of her family. Princess was fascinated with her mind reverberating and like lightening flashed back on that revolutionary moment on the bus of change, when Rose saw herself that faithful day, clutching her purse, looking out with her mind made up waiting for repercussion to face, willing to lay down her life just like Nelson Mandela, with the intent to salvaging any form of domination. Rose had always been at the frontline for equity and fairness, knowing that mistakes do occur in life.

Oftentimes many who failed, remain at that state of failure because there was no man to extend a hand of love to them. But if we must truly change, we must be ready to go out for the same cause we would want to see. When Rose saw Princess, it was obvious that something is not just right. This moment to her was never spontaneous for no Lion responds to futility, hence a calculation and timely action is required. Mindset is a set of responsibility given to us to do anything we want but whether the action is right or wrong, time would tell. Everything possible first come through our mind and then plays out to bring the change we want to see. Oftentimes we want a change we are not prepared to pay for and we often end up as if in a fog, taking the unthinkable, accepting the unacceptable, adapting to injustices, rewired to atrocities without understanding the end.

Rose did not only remain concerned for what to do to help her friend Princess; she went further to do what she wants to be remembered for. Her responsibility was laid bare, first to her friend, her family and her future. This to her was a description of change and how such change should comes is not without sacrifice and at the same time not with folding of hands in the fear of the unknown, even when the unknown is being revealed. But since she does not know the level of damage incurred by the actions of her friend, she must be willing to play by the gallery to enable Princess open up for the solution she would offer her. This is to make firm the saying that 'Humans are like mask, you do not get to know the inside until you remove the outside. The outside could sometimes contain the content entirely different from the content inside.

But on the contrary to this assertion, Rose through her actions displayed what she was inside. The effect of this action was a relief to Princess who felt all hope is lost until Rose came her way. This is to show that truly Saviors are in human form. This would be change in the life of Princess which Rose was becoming instrumental to, was from a willing heart who may not be strong, influential, a politician or a pastor but who through the unfathomable confidence and courage garnished with a little kindness, compassion, commitment and inward drive will incessantly, forcefully revealed the new meaning of possibility.

Coming to limelight is very possible for people who were consistent in the little things that would finally result in an eye-catching end. The things that matter in life are little things, which through consistency grew into mighty things. What Rose took as a small thing eventually became the beginning of the saving grace for Princess and hence was recognized as a lady who fought for a cause and conquered. Her unspoken actions to Princess brought the needed reorientation, leaving Princess passionate to make a turn in the right direction when the time comes. It is sure that the lives of many are dependent on some people who did not take time to understand the place of relevance through commitment. Rose lived her life to help those who have given up on life to gain direction. She sold herself out to help liberate those who think that their ugly past could hinder their bright future. She was a glistering star and constellation of sacrificial stars that starred forward the boat of change on the long stony road of life. From the statement of Princess, she said that many people keep looking for the next Rose to come and solve their problems and save them from their own responsibility to act, which like a web has beclouded many.

Rose laid down her life for the larger whole and was willing to die for their sake. Being a trained cohort of civil right leadership and a mentor, putting infrastructure together, Rose was waiting for the right time to bring the needed change the entire people who have given up on life was crying for. The story was that of a young quiet lady, who possibly rose against the tides of life through her character to save many people. She was willing to help, meek but no weak, quiet but not stupid and acted calculatedly and that helped to also salvage the situation of Princess, who later converted her liabilities into assets after the death of her father. Princess decided not to settle for complacency but have from that very day she met Rose fought against things she never loved in her life and that became the beginning of the breaking point for her. Rose may not have given Princess a letter of employment but she gave her a new mindset to develop. She may not have given her money but encouragement and ingenuity to rise again. She may not have recommended her, but commended her hard work and sincerity to look out for solutions.

Rose got the needed transformation and such was her life from the day she discovered purpose. She was not gender weak, the excuse many people use to limit the abilities they have, especially women who think they will end up under a man even if they do not work hard. The level of mediocrity in the world today is quite obvious that many do not know the power at their disposal to cause the most needed changes around them. They wait and wail without knowing what to do to cause the change in the environment they live. We cannot truly know what we can do until we begin to do them. We may not see strength until we stop looking at our weaknesses, which can hinder our advancement in life. A savior is needed at any point where we limit our ability to reaching the peak of life and begin to make out excuses to failure. Rose was a lady but that was not a deterrent for her to add value to people she came in contact with and from that very day, Princess learnt not to stop aiming high because of the tides of life. Rose was out to correct the wrong belief that women are only good at procreation, not as an asset. Combining work and her attitude to life brought Rose to relevance and ended her search for pearl. There are obviously many things Princess could learn from her, which includes being able to convert seeming ugly situation into an opportunity but she was certainly waiting for the right time. Princess left the scene back to her house since she could not think of anything else, optimistic and ready to be the change she wants to see but only time would tell. She raised her flag to fight and refuse to give up. As she got to her house, her mother had prepared the evening meal for the whole house. Though they have been worried lately over her plights but only time would tell how much they would hope for a better life. Princess got home that day pondering over all that her friend Rose told her. How would she transform the bulk of information into actions? As her heart ran through different things the whole night, she knew that her breakout time is near and she would soon make her family proud.

CHAPTER EIGHTEEN

THE FAMILY AND THE NEW DAWN

Princess awoke first. It took her a minute to get her bearings in the unfamiliar realities, unexpected occurrences around her and the realities the world is unveiling. Then she saw her brother and then remembered her parent with a start. Quickly looking around the little cottage, and not seeing them, she shook her brother to wake him.

"Wake up, she said to her brother. *Where is daddy? Did you see him leave?"*

Her brother quickly sat up, wiping his eyes. Then he tried to remember the events of the previous days and then came cascading down upon his still wondering mind. They have always been used to their parent doing everything for them. They have never taken time to understand the importance of all the admonition and hence the saying that we do not know the importance of anything we have until we cannot enjoy such a thing again.

Glancing around with no idea of what to do, his brother shouted.

"We had better go search for them outside."

We come to appreciate the importance of the family when they are no longer closer to us, which actually begins a new dawn. It can only be a new dawn if the instructions and trainings we were given were truly heeded. We often forget where we come from when nobody is there to guild our path.

Quickly gathering, getting set to go look for the source they believed would always be there to supply the needs, Princess and her brother started to bolt through the door as they are set to look for their parents.

Princess looked out to discover her daddy coming from a distance like a man who had set out very early.

Very happy at the sight of her daddy who had always been available for her and her siblings

As her daddy drew near, Princess was the first person to reply, *"Daddy we have been looking for you and mummy,"*

"I hope that we are not putting much pressure on you and mummy with our welfare?"

"No, you will never bother me with too much. I enjoyed them because that is why I am still alive and privileged to bring you to this world."

Princess wondered at what parenting could be like from the reply she got. The act of parenting is what makes families unique and exceptional. Everyone can give up on a person but not when such person is a member of the family although some may dare. Unfortunately some, who dared traded their family for pleasures and friends only to forget that friends could stick around as long as it is all rosy and when it becomes thorny, they would certainly back off.

"I had gone to get food before your mother and I set out for the duty of the day and to also see if we could get some money for the day's spending before we come back from today's activities".

Daddy, how long will you continue to do this?" Princess mumbled, feeling so bad that her parents could actually keep toiling to ensure they are comfortable even at their age.

The daddy seemed to disregard Princess's remark, and continued.

"Life draws so many lessons that must never be ignored. The road to being comfortable in life is never as clear as we would love it to be but we must ensure we clear the parts to access the road".

That stuck a cord in the heart of Princess who had never heard her father utter such words about life. All the while she was growing up, she had never thought life to be hard at least the celebrities she had watched all her life, never posit that life could be thorny especially when the vital essence of life is blatantly neglected. Such neglects could be as a result of not preparing well enough to face the realities of life. Life is indeed a parable.

The dominion mandate is not near reached until the fighting spirit of a giant is alive but that is not without the help of a family as first point of call for direction and guidance. Such directions as it come open up doors of possibilities when heeded in sincerity.

Stunned, Princess quickly interjected, *"Daddy, we have always watched people who never seem to have any hard time facing life. Please do not make us see otherwise."*

The father looked up at Princess and asked patiently,

"Do you not know that the seed you sow is the same to expect doing harvest?"

Princess and her brother looked at each other, and then she answered, *"Yes we know"*! Then her father said, *"It is not enough to desire the pearls of life as well as a bumper harvest, there are sacrifices that must be put in place for the expected results.* This is very true but not all sacrifices produce the right expectations.

Princess and her brother pondered this for a while and wondered such sayings from their father at a time such as this. They were surprise at what life entails and such bitter truth could not come any better and from any person than their parents. At least they could learn from the experiences of their parents never to repeat the mistakes they made. They may not have learnt the other side of life but it is good they learn that life sometimes is not fair to the fair ones. There are both sides to life, which unfortunately many do not come to appreciate early in life. Such unexpected reality dawned on them suddenly and overwhelmed them. Many who were not expecting the bitter side of life are often the victims of the realities of life. They never expected such and hence never prepared for it.

One stunning truth that I know is the fact that a day will come when we will all live to see our parents no more and then it will be totally revealed what we have learnt when they were with us, which have prepared us for the rainy days. The days are coming when the sayings of men would become a memory in the minds of those living. The days when distant become everlasting and tears are no longer enough to bring back their presence. People whose wisdom surpasses the earthly understanding are people who prepare for such days because wisdom is justified by her seeds. It is the indwelling of wisdom that makes a man to know what to do and do them.

Princess knew that the discussion is getting emotional

"After being with you and mummy, we will never be satisfied with normal lives again. And now that we have known you as our father and mummy as our mother, how can we build a lead a normal life without the presence of you and mummy? We have come to love you and appreciate your sacrificial seed of greatness, which you have always wished we harvest, we have always believed that greatness is the thing of the mind, but to think of not having you and mummy around us forever is a thought we cannot ever imagine."

Beckoning them to sit down, the father continued,

"Understand that a day will come when you will look for us to run the errands, to take the sacrifices, to get all your needs supplied and will not see me nor your mother. At that time, you will do all these things yourself. As we are getting older, we are getting closer to exit the earth when these sacrifices would be no more upon us to take. Until then, you must be able to stand up to the game of life, understand it and master the rules. Even when you may not understand the rules but you must stand up for it. You must learn to engage life until you master it. You may not win all but try to win some and win enough to keep you till death. Do not think that you know enough so as not to keep learning because any time you stop learning, you set a deliberate step to fail. Real men are empowered to confront life with actions and active participation on the things that concern and determine their existence. You must learn to observe the right protocols and love people around you. That will give you the ability and strength to face the challenges the society offer."

Princess and her brother were visibly relieved though with mixed feelings but they knew that when their father said they would one day stay in the whole earth without them, it meant they must learn to brace up and take the bull by the horn and face life totally without fear. That cannot be without the requisite sacrifice they would need to make to be able to compete favorably. They must also be given a chance to express their inert potentials, which possibly have been allowed to fallow. It also meant that they must shun evil associations that would trigger mediocrity in them.

As the three sat talking, their mother who had been away all these while came in. She was amazed at how casual these two were with their father and how casual he was with them. It is not that such moment was not seen before but not in the mood she saw them. That suggested that some things have transpired between them but what that were, remained unknown to her. Even more amazing was that He seemed to enjoy such casual moment with his children. Such causal talk to a distressed Princess and her brother could only suggest that the breaking of a new dawn is set to occur. This was something she had never seen or even considered but such must happen. It is gradually becoming obvious that age is no longer on the side of their parents. Princess had graduated since without a job and not knowing the right step to follow. The truth she had never realized was soon becoming obvious.

As they were all gathered, they began to notice some changes and different reactions coming up. Princess and her brother looked astonished as they watched their parents especially their father.

"I know you are wondering why I said all these things. It is true you have not heard these words like this since you were born but I said all these because of the beginning of the new dawn."

"True," Princess Mother replied. *At a certain time in history, we also came to the earth through the womb of our parents to begin a new order. We took over from our parents who were at one time running the errand for the family. They were there in times of sacrifice for our welfare and all these they did not counting the cost, but they kept on reminding us that a day would come when we will not see them do all these things they did for us. These things we have done today and the level of our successes in life were not because we inherited assets from them but we learnt how to obey the right principles of life and how to associate with the right people to learn every day and it paid off on the long run. We did not need to follow people around because the character of a man makes a way for him and brings him before kings. Your father and I would not have been where we are today if not for the principles of life we decided to heed."*

Such words of wisdom were enough to activate the right consciousness to pursue early the right principles of life and be better equipped with the different sides of life. How it rang in the wandering mind of Princess who was already lost at this point waiting to note the next step. What is worth doing is certainly worth doing well.

All of them were keenly listening as their mother spoke, and their father was nodding to be sure that it is going down well with his children.

Princess remembered a particular time when their father was showering them with the best life could offer as far as basic needs are concern. They had all they needed but never knew that life is not always rosy.

This is the beginning of the new dawn.

This kind of heart to heart open conversation was necessary to start preparing them for the search for relevance. Such preparation would enhance transformation in them and indeed in our children and that in turn will trigger a deep work for restructuring of the mind, their association and the environment. All these would enable them to accommodate the essence of life and the pursuits thereof. They must begin to prepare their hearts, making it receptive of good virtues while abhorring bad virtues, raising vessels that are able to attract the pearls of life.

It is not about trying to force them to live the kind of life we would want them to live but gradually guiding them to see the real sense of life. This real sense is seen when we appropriate the real values of life that would bring about the best things of life.

"We are all in the school to learn about the things we needed to know and learning about life is an entirety of what we do as we live each second of our lives. It is wisdom to be diligent in these lessons. To pass the courses of life bring more joy since the results would always be visible to all. Even though these lessons could be of a great mystery to us at the start, the joy in a man who has mastered the lessons is wonderful to behold. There is a cloud of darkness which may tend to pull men away from their pursuits in life but the persistency and the knowledge of what we could get pressing forward far outweighs the pains of drawing back.

Such understanding often leaves us focus to attaining success whether it comes when we want it or later.

The father of Princess was sitting as he gazed over his family; his other two sons who were not around these while the whole discussions began joined them. He then turned towards Princess who was beginning to walk down the narrow road of life.

Suddenly, the mountains themselves seemed to disappear in a great flash as the curtain is almost drawn to usher in the new dawn. One spectacular thing about family is the glory it brings when united. Soon the curtain shall be drawn and the glory shall be revealed coming from their parents and such spectacle was not often witnessed.

As the words of her father tapered off Princess knew the reason. A cloud is about to smile on them but not with joy in their heart. With such a great love the parents of Princess have discharged their constitutional duty over their children. The lack of this understanding have killed so many families leaving many in regrets over their inabilities to play the right role of a family. Many have often thought that the love for power is the route to success. The truth is that the love for power will often lead to a fall but when we utilize power for the sake of love, we use it rightly. The use of force in the family to communicate matters breeds fear among the members of the family but perfect love cast away fear. The reason is that with love, the greatest force of power is subdued. The use of force should be better deployed in revealing the power of love, which would enable children follow the admonitions of their parents and not doing it out of fear. This is enough to bring about right transformations.

When Princess observed her father and after watching him speak what seems to be a mystery, she said,

"Father, you have stunned me today with wisdom beyond comprehension. If only I had known these before my graduation, I would have been better for it. I am beginning to understand the reason why I am at this level. I would have grown in wisdom if I had observed your ways and deeds." Princess replied, her eyes glistering with emotion like that of her parents. *"I have learned to value the honor of beholding your ways and how you have prepared for life even more than we did, the care and love you showered on me and my siblings. I am glad watching you a satisfied man who feels contented with the little you have and I can attest that is the way to go. I understand that I wallowed in ignorance because I felt I could grasp all there is to life, watching my friends live the way they did. I have also walked amiss trying to walk right because I did not take time to master the things I have observed from you, said Princess."*

"You are wise, my daughter," Princess Father replied.

"You were all in the world at this time with me for a purpose and the reason for this time is made manifest. You are at this state because you never took time to understudy the ways and acts of

great men. But you must always remember this day and understand it so you could live a satisfied and fulfilled life after you have laid hold on the pearls. Even when you take decisions and follow your hearts, you must learn to do it for the right reasons, which you are learning now. But you must understand the relevance of being productive and engaging the truths you now know even as I go the way of all men."

The father continue,

"I want to give you the last secret to the pearls of life but first of all, you must commit to watching to the things of utmost importance. You must be someone who listens if you truly want the treasures of life to heed to your call. You must master how to care for things and people around you, that is the only way to be loved. When you care, show it through giving and blessings would come knocking at your door. Never leave the faint-hearted without comfort, if you truly want to enjoy peace. Wisdom is shown through understanding and you must seek to understand how things function and why you take every decision in life. Kind-hearted people always attract destiny helpers not those with beautiful body. Learn to value truths and men will respect you any day. Actions to be taken today must not be procrastinated else you

will halt your advancement. Do not seek to bring people down, if you want to remain relevant and on the top. Do not forget the place of gratitude with the little you have if you wish to get things in bountiful measure. Create an environment filled with joy to shine as light for others. Do not be afraid to face challenges, whether big or small as it enhances your personal growth. Life is a series of problem-solving opportunities to make a difference in the society. You can either be developed or defeated depending on your response to challenges. Many react negatively to challenges and resent their problems rather than pausing to consider what benefit are ahead of them."

With these words, as they all watched, the father of Princess breathed his last and as they watched him, they discovered he is gone. What a way to exit the earth. With these words, Princess brazed up and had a total change of orientation as to what life should be. These are like words on a marble and she went out with the energy that exhumed from these words to make a difference. Few months after the burial of her father, she got employed into the same multinational firm, her friend Rose works with. Her ethical and proficient prowess was so much that she was promoted as one of the company's director and the son of the manager of the company noticed her hard work and beauty of character, which she began to portray and proposed to her and they got married and lived happily ever after. The long awaited pearls of life and all the dreams Princess had was eventually fulfilled, with her history rewritten forever. Princess gave birth to two wonderful children and her husband loved her and she was treated as the queen she was.

The End

EPILOGUE

Life operates through Principles. Africa is the way it is not because we lack resources for the development but because Principles are neglected. The leaders have competence but much more is required. Every day we face hundreds of decisions to make. We are pulled; we are distracted, and sometimes even in our best moments, yet we do not get what is ultimate. Even focusing on experiencing success is one step short of focusing on the things that lead to success. So neither success nor influence is ultimate, character is. We can get enamored with a telescope and forget to see the object at which it is pointed. The mission is that the knowledge of good character will cover the earth as the water covers the sea. Character not affluence is the scarce resource that is in constant demand to get the good things of life.